The Moral Manager

Samuel M. Natale
John B. Wilson
Linda S. Perry

Studies in Business and Economics
Global Publications, Binghamton University
Binghamton, New York

Copyright © 2002 by Samuel M. Natale, John B. Wilson, and Linda S. Perry

All rights reserved. No portion of this publication may be duplicated in any way without the expressed written consent of the publisher, except in the form of brief excerpts or quotations for the purposes of review.

Library of Congress Cataloging-in-Publication Data

Natale, Samuel M.
   The moral manager / Samuel M. Natale, John B. Wilson, Linda S. Perry.
      p. cm. -- (Studies in business and economics)
   ISBN 1-58684-210-2 (pbk. : alk. paper)
   1. Business ethics. 2. Executives--Professional ethics. 3. Industrial management--Moral and ethical aspects. 4. Executives--Training of. I. Wilson, John, 1928- II. Perry, Linda S. III. Title. IV. Series: Studies in business and economics (Binghamton, N.Y.)
   HF5387 .N363 2002
   174'.4--dc21
                                                                2002006788

Published by Global Publications
Binghamton University, State University of New York
Binghamton, New York, USA 13902-6000
Phone: (607) 777-4495. Fax: 777-6132
E-mail: pmorewed@binghamton.edu
http://ssips.binghamton.edu

For Gayle R. Rapp
  ∼ a friend for all seasons

Contents

Foreword vii

Acknowledgements xiii

Introduction 1

Chapter One: The Psychological Background to
    Moral Eduction 9

Chapter Two: Morals For Manager 43

Chapter Three: Morality, Management, and Passion . . .63

Chapter Four: A Business Perspective on Ethics and
    Morals 81

Chapter Five: Universal Moral and Ethical Education,
    Cultural Approaches, and A Roadmap for the Moral
    Manager in Applying Business Ethics 117

Index 171

About the Authors 183

Foreword

As someone who has been in the business world for more than 22 years, I found myself a bit nervous when approaching a book with the title, *The Moral Manager*. Don't get me wrong, I've worked with some wonderfully moral and principled people throughout the years, and I consider myself to be moral and principled, but we all know of the "war stories" that exist about "the others."

All organizations have a culture or, if you prefer, a personality. Very often "buzz words" or a lingo are part of that culture. Morality is not a word one hears on a daily basis in the business world/workplace. The "bottom line," "profitability," "sales volume," "revenues," "gross margin"— all of these, certainly. More recently words such as teamwork, leadership, empowerment, motivation, coaching, respect, and caring are commonplace in business. It may well be that morality is at the root of the inclusion of the more recent terminology with those that have always been a driving factor in any business's success and longevity. We have some work to do to bring the words morality, principles, morals, and ethics into everyday discussions in the workplace – to make it more evident to ourselves and others that we operate in this way.

We must not deem today's workplaces as dens of inequity or places where morals do not exist—morality does exist, and it plays a role in the functioning of a business (although the recent Enron activities force us to wonder why that particular business environment seemed to have it in such short supply!). Surely, most managers consider the repercussions of the decisions we make: how will this impact the profitability of the enterprise **and** what the effect will be on the people it touches—our human resources, our customers, our vendors, our competitors, etc. And if the latter will be damaged in some significant way, the former does not always hold sway. Potentially difficult situations do arise, and appropriate decisions are made frequently based on the morals of those in authority.

Just as organizations have a culture or a "personality," so do the individuals that make up the organization; this means a substantial number of differing values also exist, or coexist. That being the case, it would make sense to develop a common language for the moral actions we take in business, make it a part of our daily conversations at work, and instill it as part of the culture. Since there are many values operating in the workplace, the training in this common language and its application to our daily decision-making would help clarify the meaning of morality and bring home the message that it is expected in the workplace. Just as the words margins, revenues, etc. are part of the daily routine, so should be the words values, justice, honesty, respect, morals, and morality.

At Symbol Technologies, we tie our core values and code of conduct to performance evaluation. Our core values include:

>Customer Satisfaction
>
>Continuous Improvement
>
>Management by Fact
>
>Teamwork
>
>Innovation
>
>Caring

Our Code of Conduct performance factors are:

>Respect Others
>
>Assume Accountability/Share Authority
>
>A "Can Do" Associate
>
>Questions/Participates
>
>Meeting Participation
>
>Listens Constructively

Performance is vitally important, of course, but what is also critical is **how** you achieve the results. Measuring individual performance against the core values and code of conduct provides us the opportunity to discuss how we exemplify them in the workplace – how we are "walking the walk and talking the talk." They are more than words, they are an integral part of the way we do business and conduct ourselves on a daily basis.

There is still work to be done in organizations on this topic. Educators can help by providing the "context" for morality through case studies, as well as working with students to help them understand what "tools" will be needed to function morally and ethically in life's tougher situations—professional or personal. We're not speaking of "preaching" here, but of real in-depth study of morals and morality and the impact on people throughout the ages, of deep discussions of how, when, and why taking the moral high road worked and what happened when the low road was taken. Children today want the adults to ensure they will have a healthy planet on which they can grow up; a look back at decisions that were made where the high road was the best choice, but not the road taken, could be part of the moral education process. It helps provide the "context" in a way that should be relative and understandable.

We in the workplace can help by continuing the process begun by the educators. In addition to creating a more profound understanding of ethics and morals at work, it can be extremely valuable to our decision-making and problem-solving training programs. These programs are also useful for building teamwork and community and can bring about a closer alignment of individual and company values, all very worthwhile goals for any organization. If we educate and train people in this way, incorporate words such as morals and morality and integrity and ethics into our everyday discussions with personnel, customers, vendors, competitors,

Foreword

etc., add these to our Mission Statements if they are not already there, we truly create a common language with a strong message: Ethics and morality are at work here.

Carole DeMayo

Sr. Vice President of Human Resources
Symbol Technologies, Inc.

Acknowledgements

We owe a profound debt of gratitude to the Department of Educational Studies, University of Oxford as well as the Oxford University Centre for the Study of Values in Education and Business which permitted us the opportunity to explore many of these ideas more fully in postgraduate seminars to incorporate their critical feedback.

We are also deeply grateful to the business executives who made themselves available to discuss the varied implications of Moral Education in the day-to-day workplace unprotected by academic tranquility.

Special gratitude goes to Dr. Parviz Morewedge for his interest and care in moving this book from a series of discussions to a final unified work.

A large debt. is owed to Katherine Ensor Pueschel for her detailed, energetic and incisive editorial questions and suggestions. Often she was clearer in understanding what we were trying to say that we ourselves were.

Acknowledgements

Finally, we are grateful to Ellen Wynn for her unending availability, upbeat response to often frantic last-minute changes and a general sense of professionalism throughout the entire process.

Introduction

Manager. We've all heard the title applied in a variety of different ways. Today, it's a simple matter to call up a job search engine such as Monster.com or Hot Jobs.com and enter the word. The responses range from low-paid entry-level positions with no authority to highly-paid, responsibility-rich careers.

The fact is that the word manager has become a catch-all term for someone who *manages* a process or people. In this book, we are interested in individuals who *manage* people. This is the crux of the moral manager — how he or she interacts with both the people who work for him or her and the company itself.

A real manager is a facilitator, someone who satisfactorily completes a task. In a perfect world, the manager issues orders outlined by senior management to the employees, or *direct reports*. The manager applies and enforces the company's rules, which one might expect to involve application of black-and-white principles. For example, managers learn how to deal with absenteeism, tardiness, theft, lying, and workplace conflict. Managers also learn how to rate employees, reward those who surpass expectations and punish those who don't meet expectations.

Unfortunately, the manager's workplace is not a perfect world and managing people is not a simple job; the moral manager is often required to do a balancing act between meeting the requirements of the business and protecting and nurturing his or her direct reports. When, as often happens, the workers are in opposition to management, making a judgement about what course of action to pursue will likely involve difficult ethical questions. When enforcing company standards, how does a manager apply those standards to senior managers? They may very well be engaged in less than perfect conduct. And how does a manager deal with a company-wide problem — say defrauding clients, cheating the government, selling shoddy or dangerous products, or polluting the environment? What happens when company policy is in opposition to a manager's personal sense of morality?

Indeed, bottom-up policing has always been a rather "iffy" proposition, especially in companies that have no means for communicating problems that come from above. Imagine trying to blow the whistle on a senior manager you report to, without having a way to leapfrog up the chain of command. Even when there are mechanisms in place for voicing concerns, they are often handled carelessly, with the end result that the complainer develops a bad reputation that can affect his or her career. These are real-life issues that have always been part and parcel of a manager's life.

Introduction

MANAGEMENT THROUGH HISTORY

Management has always been with us. The earliest tribal units probably had some type of governing body, either a matriarch or patriarch who suggested courses of action. Generally, the people who were good at something would be the leader. The best hunter might lead a hunting party, the best warrior would manage war activities. Many native American tribes had different "experts" who led by example; Sitting Bull for example, was a religious leader.

However, leading by example meant that when a subordinate disagreed, he or she was free to ride off on his/her own, because there was no concept of desertion.

Studying rigidly hierarchical societies teaches us that subordinates didn't have it so easy. Roman soldiers served for 20 years; desertion was punished by death and decimation was a tool always available to senior management. In Ancient Egypt, overseers whipped the slaves who built the pyramids. (Slaves as employees offered management fewer bargaining problems, but presented a lasting moral quagmire).

Leaping ahead to the Industrial Revolution, management as we know it began to evolve. Here, non-agricultural pursuits in mines and factories began to create the distinct employer/employee dichotomy. Employers wanted as low an overhead as possible to create products that could be sold at a high profit. That's been the equation ever since.

Unfortunately, employees died by the thousands in mines. They also became affected by many previously unknown ailments, and worked very long hours for very little pay. In this environment, first-line management was an escape to a far better life and away from the hand-to-mouth existence of many workers.

The great reforms of our civilization have arisen from this contention between workers and management. From Marxism and Socialism and Capitalism all the way to Fascism, the relationship of workers and employers is at the heart of the key issues. Interestingly enough, the twentieth century's great wars were between competing ideologies and the participants became part of industry as soon as the wars ended. Looking back to the late 40's and early 50's, management positions were often filled by former military officers; this made perfect sense, since classical business management structures often reflected the military hierarchy. First-line managers were lieutenants and captains; middle managers were majors and colonels; and senior management was the realm of generals.

However, military hierarchy is unwieldy, not to mention unfair. On the battlefield, orders are given and instant obedience is demanded. The argument is that unless subordinates follow orders blindly, the "grand plan" will fall apart. There are, of course, two ways of looking at this argument. Management never likes to be questioned, especially in matters of strategy. The "big picture" is what concerns managers, and they consider that subordinates cannot be expected to understand all the details of a grand operation, so they need only to do their own job and be content that the orders given are appropriate.

Unfortunately, as one looks through the confused haze of military operations historically, incompetence and bloody-

Introduction

mindedness are rife. One would hardly blame a WW I infantryman ordered out of the safety of the trenches and into the path of enemy artillery and machine-gun fire if he thought his superiors may not have had a lot on the ball. In fact, some French troops actually mutinied because of the slaughter of World War I.

The truth is that management superiors may be too far removed from the daily work, with the result that orders received below don't make any sense. In war, for instance, orders might be given to cross a minefield or direct artillery fire at a town already taken. In business, workers might be assigned duplicate tasks or be ordered into an unsafe work situation, for example, to enter a dangerous mine. This is another area that demands attention by the moral manager: communication from top to bottom, and back up again, must also be efficiently managed. In business, accurate, timely information is worth its weight in gold and the manager must be in position to paint a detailed picture of operations for his or her superiors as well.

Today, the hierarchies are flattening, and the CEO is now much closer to the actual work than ever before. That's simply because no modern organization can afford slow turn-around times. Customer relationship management, or CRM, demands responsiveness. In the age of online shopping and online b-to-b and b-to-c operations, no business can afford to alienate customers; they always have alternatives they can rapidly exploit.

Similarly, in this era of high competition for the best workers, businesses can't afford problems with employees. In fact, employee turnover can cripple enterprises — which, in turn, places more pressure on management to deal less harshly and more creatively with their workforce.

These are the modern pressures on the moral manager: dealing with intelligent, questioning employees who can leave any minute for better positions; and dealing with superiors who may or may not be in touch with the actual needs of the company — or may not be in compliance with normal, ethical standards.

On top of all this, we have the new phenomenon of the dot-com organization. Small, fast-paced, VC-funded, and generally based on a killer application, these new firms are in some ways a throwback to the past. The twenty- and thirty-some-year-old wunderkind often goes through workers faster than the old coal mine did (though with less drastic results). Both employee relations and customer relations are primitive at best. Within these companies, there is a sense that employees are pulling together, working 18-hour days for the good of the business (with the eternal hope that stock options will reward hard work). Recent economic shakeups have put out some of the fire, but the generally rudimentary employee-relations techniques put an extra strain on management.

THE FUTURE

In this book we'll explore the development of the moral manager; the training, expectations and pressures that define the problems and solutions of moral management. We'll delve into the environment that produces both managers and

Introduction

employees and the different issues that face all of us from a moral standpoint. We'll look at moral management from a company-wide perspective and we'll offer some solid guidelines to acting as a moral manager in all situations. And we'll add a dimension generally not discussed in conjunction with management — passion. Passion for the job and passion for the process.

Basically, *management* boils down to people — how to manage subordinates and how to influence the business' decision makers. However, that covers a lot of ground, and managers today need to be everything from process experts to confessors. The moral manager should know his or her people and be accessible. As well, the moral manager owes his or her loyalty to the business and a day's work for a day's pay.

This is where the seeds of conflict are and always will be sown. In our fast-paced world, managers must make snap decisions that will affect lives and profits. There will always be repercussions for bad or distant management; these can range from common employee dissatisfactions to instances of aggrieved employees mowing down co-workers and superiors with semi-automatic rifle fire.

In this book, we will tackle the many issues that confront today's manager and offer a guide to successfully navigating between the employee rock and the business hard place.

Chapter One
The Psychological Background to Moral Education

The first step to moral management is moral education. How are managers shaped by their backgrounds? How are they defined by their understanding of authority?

Our first step on the path of defining the moral manager is to clarify the basic logic or philosophy of moral education. We believe, however, that whether or not any such rational basis will actually be put to educational use depends centrally upon our attitude toward certain basic concepts, in particular that of *authority*. The logical or rational position has been explored in earlier work (see Wilson 1977); but we need to understand *why* this position is resisted. How, in fact, *do* (not *ought*) we think or feel about authority?

We say "How do *we* think about it, but who are *we*? It is important to realize that there are significant differences between different individuals and groups, and to appreciate those differences. The most basic and easily identifiable difference consists in whether a person or group is *for* or *against* authority in general:

1. The first position involves *identification* with authority. Here the individual (or the society as a whole) sees himself as the unquestionable representative of a corpus of truths and values. He has the "right answers," and his job is to pass these on to his pupils so that they believe and act in accordance with them. Confident in this assumption, he welcomes the power, authority, sanctions, and disciplinary measures deemed necessary to put it into practice. The authority may be described or rationalized in different ways, as "Marxist ideology," "a Christian way of life," "British (French, etc.) culture and traditions," "middle-class values," or whatever. This posture is visible, in extreme forms, in totalitarian and authoritarian societies, though of course, it is not confined to them.

2. The second position involves *rejection* of authority. Here the individual is in a state of reaction against whatever he takes to be current authorities ("the establishment"). He does not regard his own beliefs and values as having priority over others' beliefs and values, or as forming a firm and secure basis for education: he may indeed adopt some kind of relativist position in which the objectivity of truth and a system of values are themselves called into question or even denied. He is likely to favor a non-hierarchical ideology and some

The Psychological Background to Moral Education

kind of egalitarianism (as it were, dismantling existing authority and dissipating it throughout society) along with certain interpretations of *democracy* or *participation*; and he is likely to favor *integration* and object to some practices as *divisive* or *elitist*. This posture is more often visible in liberal societies (the UK is a fair example).

In a broad sense, these are the yin and yang of attitudes that managers will most likely face. There will be employees who blindly follow orders, and others who resent being asked to do anything.

It is fairly easy to see how each of these attitudes strays from the concept of education. On the one hand, the notion of education – indeed of learning itself – is connected with the logically basic notion of a *rational* stance toward the world. This stance is primary — items claimed as truth or knowledge or worthwhile values derive their validity from the primary concept of reasonable procedures, rather than vice versa. "Right answers" cannot be the starting point of education, since their rightness (if they are indeed right) can only be a function of the criteria of reason that justify them as right. This is perhaps most obvious in the case of moral education, where it is clear that no first-order set of values – no specific moral *content* — can be taken for granted. For such education, we have to rely on initiating pupils to an understanding of, and then training them to grasp the rational procedures which they can use to generate, their own values. Objections to indoctrination, or the socialization of pupils into norms and practices that may well be questioned, rest ultimately on this point, as do the legitimate demands under such headings as *autonomy* and *critical thinking*. In a word, the only authority an educator can ultimately recognize is the authority of reason itself, not of any particular or partisan ideology. On the other hand, to dismantle or reject authority in general, to fall into any kind of relativism, to react against the whole *concept* of "right answers," equally strays from the idea of education; for the notions of reason, learning, knowledge, truth, and hence, of education itself are connected to that concept. Rational procedures (if we can get clear about them) do not have authority, but educators can and must have authority, insofar as they act as representatives of these procedures. Educators are, for instance, representatives and teachers of how to think reasonably about the physical world (science), about the past (history), and so on. Furthermore, educators need the practical or social authority necessary to transmit these procedures to their pupils — briefly, educators need the authority and power necessary to enforce whatever discipline is required for education.

Of these two fundamental orientations to authority, there are perhaps good reasons for concentrating at the present time on the second. First, the position of *identification* with authority involves a much simpler reaction; the individual simply takes up the mantle of authority passed to him by his parents (or elders, or whomever represents "the establishment"). Second, that reaction may be regarded as, in some sense, the natural state, while the reaction of *rejection* as may be considered more complex and sophisticated, at least at the public or social level. (We do not deny that the psychic roots of rejection lie very deep, as the work of such post-Freudians as Melanie Klein shows). Third, again at a public or social level, increased communications and a wide-spread surge in the desire for *liberation* or *autonomy* – one might say generally, of "doing one's own thing" – make the first position much more difficult to sustain; to continue the traditions of an authoritarian folk society in the face of potential revolution and a desire for independence is extremely difficult in the modern world. Finally, there is some evidence (though we shall not discuss it here) that those who control and operate education in many societies, particularly in the western world, favor rejection of rather than identification with authority: for instance, in the UK, many of the most articulate and influential teachers and educators have significantly favored relativism, egalitarianism, *integration* and other ideas that characterize that rejection. These points are of course very briefly stated, and much sociological and psychological enquiry needs to be devoted to them. Further, it is of course always true that the opposite reaction, identification with authority, is always possible and will to some extent occur by a swing of the pendulum or even concurrently (for instance, dissatisfaction with "liberal" or "wishy-washy" religious and moral education may generate a desire to have one's children educated in a much more authoritarian regime, perhaps based on Christian fundamentalist principles or some other hard-line ideology; this seems to be occurring in some western democracies). Motives here are not always complex: communities and individuals have a desire for security at all costs, for a clear and hard line, have a fear of some sort of schizoid split (both in society and in the individual psyche) which can only be staved off by uncritical acceptance of a straightforward ideology, a desire for a "faith to live by," "law and order," "the preservation of standards and traditions" – all these are fairly familiar to us, and have been tolerably well documented, sometimes under headings such as the *authoritarian personality*. Rejection of authority is a more complex reaction, and deserves our more immediate attention.

AUTHORITY CONTESTED

Characteristic symptoms of rejection of authority include the following general ideas:

(a) *Education* is a contestable concept, without any fixed definition and without specific values of its own, and is therefore fundamentally an ideological notion.

(b) That there is no real distinction between educational goods, reasons and arguments on the one hand, and political or social goods, reasons and arguments on the other.

(c) "Democracy," "participation," "autonomy," and "freedom" are good; "authority," "obedience," "taking orders," and "conforming" are bad.

(d) Rules and punishment should be reduced to a minimum.

(e) Anger, aggression, competition, violence and power are bad.

(f) Teachers should not have *impersonal* authority.

(g) Examinations are bad if they make some pupils feel that they have failed.

(h) There are no things existing in their own right called "subjects," "disciplines" or "forms of thought" with their own rules and standards.

The Psychological Background to Moral Education

(i) Any form of privilege or selectivity is dangerous and immoral.
(j) In terms of innate intelligence or ability, there are no basic, non-negotiable differences between the genders, or different races, or between different types of pupils.
(k) There are no objective and demonstrably correct values.
(l) Integrating things (pupils, subjects) is good, segregating bad.

This round dozen is an arbitrary number, if only because what is designated as a symptom must relate to our views about basic causes. The connection with a reaction against authority is clear enough. It is also, we hope, clear that these symptoms do not always, perhaps not even very often, represent rational attitudes (such as, for instance, a reasonable sense of resentment at injustice); sometimes, indeed, they run into logical impossibilities – as for instance in (g), where it is clear that any form of assessment, examination or checking-up will necessarily grade some people above others (whether or not we use words like *pass* and *fail*). We do not propose here to argue philosophically against these general ideas; they are, in any case, far too general to accept or deny as they stand. We need rather to look at some of the emotions and attitudes that may underlie them.

Here we face methodological problems: how, in fact, does one verify either in oneself or other people, the operation of a particular emotion or prejudice or fantasy? At what level of the psyche are our descriptions and explanations operating, since the human mind is a complex and layered entity, in which one emotion covers up another? To what extent can we distinguish and tabulate these things, since they often act together, and to what extent should we be content with a general description that aims at giving some plausible phenomenological account rather than a proper etiology? Fortunately these matters, though faced daily by therapists and others concerned with individual psychic problems and difficulties, need not be fully discussed here: for there is, in itself a very striking fact, little or no literature (with honorable but few exceptions) which relates the work of psychoanalytic psychologists and psychiatrists to such public enterprises as education. We can hope only to give some kind of general account that other scholars with more expertise and experience can pursue.

One of the basic elements in the reaction against authority is, of course, the natural resentment that the child feels at being in the power of adults. It seems to him deeply and dangerously unfair, though at the same time he needs the support, love and discipline of the adults. There is a fear of being crushed, overpowered, dictated to, tyrannized, a fear arising simply from weakness and his dependent position. The fear naturally generates hatred and aggression toward the adults. It may also generate *envy* of their superior position and advantages, which the child wishes to see removed and abolished. So, much of the teacher's reaction against authority involves his/her identification *with the child* – that is, in effect, with the child within himself – rather than with adult authority. These are, perhaps, fairly obvious psychic features whose

The Psychological Background to Moral Education

operation in politics and elsewhere is not hard to perceive.

More subtly, there may arise from these feelings the fear of one's own aggression, and the consequent tender-minded rejection of what seems connected with an aggressive and "punitive" attitude (as in (d) and (e) above); hence the general approval of "non-violence," "a caring attitude," and perhaps the passion for conservation of species and ecology generally, together with a dislike of rules, punishments, and other features of the apparatus of authority. Feelings of *guilt* may also arise, particularly if the person has to take on an authoritative position or exercise power, and especially if he has profited from institutions connected with privilege (many teachers from well-off families who have been to "good" schools feel guilty about this, even guilty about sending their own children to such schools).

More subtle still, and hard to describe because the relevant concepts are not always marked by ordinary language, is the kind of feeling characteristic of puritanical and "leveler" movements generally. The very trappings of authority, tradition and privilege are – what shall we say? Hated? Feared? Distrusted? Consider the attitude of the Cromwellian puritans to such trappings, or of John Knox; Puritanism seems to involve some deep-rooted alarm and hatred directed against images and representations that it associates with a smug and self-complacent elite. The response is in a way aesthetic, though *moral* may catch its forcefulness better. Features which might fairly be regarded as comparatively harmless, at worst as time-wasting rituals, are nevertheless targets for very real passion: high tables at Oxbridge colleges, the wearing of gowns, the House of Lords, Latin speeches, "aristocratic" dress and accent. Safety is felt to exist only in egalitarian homogeneity, in which one who desires to exert influence must show himself to be "a man of the people," never claiming expertise or privilege or any kind of superiority.

Insofar as educators are susceptible – and in many societies they are peculiarly susceptible – to this rejection of authority, they distance themselves both from those (many) who favor the (often uncritical) acceptance of traditional authority based on the concept of education itself. In particular, they distance themselves from parents, employers, and governments who have a vested interest in the acceptance of whatever authority is needed to ensure that the young are kept under proper control, brought up to be reasonably well behaved, and given the knowledge and skills necessary for employment and the efficient running of the state. In their rejection of authority, educators cast themselves in the role of missionaries, apostles of some liberationist ideology, defenders of the underdog; they consider themselves no longer representatives of an existing set of cultural and moral values and standards (let alone those values and standards which, by their connection with rational procedures, are absolutely necessary for any serious education). A right-wing backlash, usually equally uncritical and irrational, inevitably follows.

It is noteworthy that this may well apply not only to educators but also to the "caring professions" generally, in particular to church ministry and social work. Here, too, as one might expect, and as is perhaps apparent in the remarkable shift to the left in such institutions as the Church of England,

The Psychological Background to Moral Education

the rejection of authority has affected not only the internal attitude to the norms governing the profession's own authority – the theological and administrative traditions of the Church, for instance – but also its attitude in government, society and politics. The question of what *authority* a priest, social worker, youth leader or whatever is supposed to have – what expertise he possesses which justifies his professional work – is rarely raised, because the answer approved by this reaction might well be "none at all." Even the medical profession, normally much more self-confident in its expertise, is under heavy pressure not just from *alternative medicine* but from its own fear of assuming an authoritative mantle.

The temptation at this point, one perhaps yielded to by not a few contemporary right-wing governments, is to suppose that the crisis can be overcome by some kind of central control on the part of those who do not reject authority; unfortunately, this is not only dangerous but logically impossible. It is dangerous because authoritarianism is likely to be the basis for such control, but is no better than rejection of authority. It is impossible because (as we said earlier) the educators have themselves to become more reasonable if education is to go well, and must not just accept dictation from outside. Education must – logically must – remain largely in the hands of the educators who alone (like parents) are on sufficiently intimate terms with their pupils to have any hope of making the right decisions.

Although the distinction between the two stances toward authority is important, it may be less important than a quite different distinction. We are familiar with the idea that *extremists* in both groups, like extremist Fascists and Communists, are apt to have a great deal in common. There is a distinction between extremism and moderation, fanaticism and common sense, which cuts across both reactions to authority. For the fact is that, somewhere in our minds, we feel both identification with *and* rejection of authority – that is why the pendulum swings so easily between the two reactions, between authoritarianism and chaos, totalitarianism and anarchy, a rigid and repressive use of authority and an abandonment of authority altogether. Hence, we should not be surprised if extremists start by being "against" authority but then find themselves backing a very strong authority of their own – for instance, as the Communists' enforcement of "the Party line" against the old, hated authority of the Czar and the aristocrats. The important thing, then, may be not whether we take sides between identification with and rejection of authority – we are bound to feel both of them, more or less unconsciously – but how well we manage to *deal with* both sets of feelings.

Compare, for instance, a quotation from an (unnamed) Nazi source, produced about 1938:

> *Unquestioning obedience to his parents is the duty of every German child. But that is not enough. The authorities of the State are not to be challenged – in particular the laws and the Leader, Adolf Hitler, who is divinely appointed to rule us in every way. The police must be regarded as similarly appointed: it is not the business of the ordinary citizen to question them in any way. As for those who do – in particular the Jews, and all who seek to destroy the State –*

they deserve only our hate and our fury. We shall take revenge on them, be sure of that.

But this sort of thing is present in all societies, more or less on or below the surface. Consider this report (*Daily Mirror*, 17 February, 1987): *"By 1999 the urban war will be a permanent feature of everyday life in every city…. There will be guns and death on both sides."* This is not just a prediction. It is the earnest prayer of Britain's newest group of Fascist extremists, Nazis of the left. They call themselves "Class War;" they say they are left-wing, but their aims and methods are no different from those of their right-wing foes in National Front-style gangs: violence and chaos. When the group achieves its aim, Class War will rise from the ashes to establish a new order, replacing the class system it despises.

"Last week their extremism was directed at 'East Enders' star Tom Watt when he opened a private housing development in London's East End."

Watt, "Lofty" in the TV series, is a member of the Labor Party and CND. But in a rare piece of publicity-seeking, Class War seized the opportunity to get their message across.

Menace

CW members screamed that he was a *"'Judas,' traitor to true East Enders"* for linking himself with a private-housing scheme.

Class War's leader is granny-spectacled, donkey-jacketed Ian Bone, a 40-year-old sociology graduate and son of a butler.

"'If he's a lunatic, he's a dangerous one,' says a leading member of Militant, the former black sheep of the left."

CW was founded two years ago by a handful of seasoned anarchists, and is now controlled by a secret politburo of 25 members.

The full membership and sympathizers of this growing menace are *"widely spread,"* says Bone.

Posh

The movement has two "newspapers" – *Class War* and *Angry*, which describes itself as the "theoretical journal" of the party.

Their "theory" is stated as:

Seeking to replace "the State" with a series of "self-policing" groups.

Their paper, *Class War*, said of the Brixton riots: *"the best Saturday night out in years. Bleeding brilliant. We took on the murdering fascist pigs. We confront these bastards and maim them and kill them BECAUSE WE HATE THEM."*

A member said, *"We fully admit that many of us were there and took an active part."*

Admitting that *"'only a handful of us' live in the riot areas,"* he added: *"Why shouldn't we pour in and fight among our comrades and our class?"*

Issues of *Class War* carry a regular feature called "Hospitalised Copper."

After the murder of PC Blakelock on the Broadwater

Farm estate, the publication carried a joke: *"What's the difference between a copper and a onion? Answer: You cry when you cut up an onion."*

Other *Class War* leaflets cover topics ranging from instructions on *"How to rip off the DHSS"* to appeals for the hearts and minds of the young with instructions on how to *"F*** School."*

CW sees "the Establishment" as virtually everyone bar themselves.

"'The Labor Party, CND, Militant – they are all a pathetic joke,' said one member, who preferred not to give his name."

SOME CONSIDERATIONS FROM RESEARCH

We have just looked at two general attitudes to authority and ended with an alarming and (deliberately) extreme example. If one asks normal children to say what they think about discipline and authority, much of what they say seems harmless and often sensible:

"I don't mind teachers telling me what to do if it's sensible."

"It's funny, I never liked being told what to do even if it's right."

"I rather like being told what to do; it saves you having to think."

"Why is it good to be under discipline? Isn't self-discipline much better?"

"I'd always do what Miss ____ tells me, I just think she's marvelous."

"My father's always bullied my big brother, he's just a wreck; I'm not going to be like that."

"New kids ought to have more discipline, they don't know what's good for them."

"When I have children I'm going to bring them up much more strictly."

"You need discipline to keep you on the rails."

"I don't mind discipline in playing football and that sort of thing. I'm keen on that; but in class – that's something different, it's boring."

"The discipline in our school is far too strict, silly rules about uniforms and things like that. What's it matter what you wear?"

But we can perhaps detect in these children's responses, as in our own thinking, tendencies to extremism that we have to watch. It is not too far a step from the school bully to the member of the National Front who bullies racial minorities. We do not intend to suggest that *normal* children are any more to be watched than *normal* adults (there are plenty of horror stories to be told about both). But we desperately need to understand the roots of our feelings more deeply and in more detail. With this in mind, we and some colleagues interviewed several hundred people to find out how they thought about discipline and authority in schools; we were particularly interested in attitudes about discipline, since this (we guessed) was the way in which the idea of authority impinged on them most directly. We divided our respondents into four groups: (A) pupils of secondary-school age, (B) parents of pupils at secondary schools, (C) teachers at secondary schools, and (D) educational theorists and administrators. We then compiled a list of twenty questions, based on what seemed to be the most relevant features of discipline and authority. The questions were in three groups, as follows:

> I. *Conceptual clarity.* Here we were concerned only with respondents' logical or conceptual grasp. These questions were (for reasons given earlier) perhaps the most important, but we did not usually ask them first; to do so, we found, tended to inhibit the respondents, who responded as if they were being asked some sort of examination question. The questions were:
>
> 1. Did the respondent grasp that discipline had to do with obedience?
> 2. Did the respondent grasp that discipline had to do with obedience to legitimate authority as such (not for any old reason)?
> 3. Did the respondent grasp the necessity ("value") of discipline in schools?
> 4. Did the respondent grasp the necessity ("value") of discipline in life generally?

5. Did the respondent grasp the need for rules backed by sanctions?
6. Did the respondent grasp the need for the authority's legitimacy and power for *educational* purposes only?

II. *Empirical fact.* Here we were concerned with views on what was, or would under certain circumstances be, the case. These questions were:

7. Was discipline adequately understood in most schools?
8. Was it adequately enforced?
9. Was lack of enforcement due to lack of nerve and clarity, or other factors?
10. Would parents willingly contract to have discipline adequately enforced?
11. Would pupils willingly contract to have discipline adequately enforced?
12. Did pupils prefer existing disorder to more discipline?
13. Given the present state of the law, could discipline be adequately enforced?

III. *Suggestions for improvement.* Here we were concerned with some rather obvious suggestions, which they might or might not endorse. These questions were:

14. Should sanctions (of whatever kind) be sufficiently strong to ensure obedience?
15. Should teachers be trusted with the power to operate these sanctions?
16. Should there be a right of appeal by pupils against teachers, at least in some cases?

The Psychological Background to Moral Education

17. Should rules, contracts, and sanctions be clearly and fully spelled out in schools?
18. Should the head teacher have more or less ultimate authority in matters of discipline?
19. Should some disciplinary powers be delegated to "prefects" or other selected pupils?
20. Should there be more attention paid to discipline and authority (in contrast with other educational objectives, e.g., academic or vocational knowledge and skill).

We do not want here either to discuss fully the methodological problems of this sort of research, or to present the research as having "proved" anything in any "scientific" way. Nevertheless, the results were interesting. We give on the following pages the percentages of people in each of the four groups who seemed to us (after lengthy interviews and discussions with each individual) to have entertained certain concepts and beliefs, and to have been willing to make certain prescriptions, in response to the questions above.

Specified responses (percentages)

Key: A: Pupils
      B: Parents
      C: Teachers
      D: Educationalists

		A	B	C	D
I:	Grasp of:				
1.	Discipline as obedience	73	81	56	24
2.	Obedience to legitimate authority as such	55	73	31	16
3.	Necessity for discipline in schools	91	98	85	53
4.	Necessity for discipline in life generally	87	97	93	43
5.	Need for rules backed by sanctions	91	99	71	34
6.	Legitimate authority for purposes of education only	94	47	53	41

	A	B	C	D
II: Belief that:				
7. Discipline not adequately understood in schools	94	99	31	30
8. Discipline not adequately enforced in schools	90	99	65	41
9. Lack of enforcement chiefly due to lack of nerve and clarity	89	98	16	31
10. Parents would contract for enforcement	93	91	43	30
11. Pupils would contract for enforcement	83	73	38	27
12. Pupils did not prefer existing disorder	100	74	63	13
13. Discipline enforceable in existing state of law	91	98	31	30
III: Prescription that:				
14. Sanctions be strong enough to ensure obedience	98	99	63	43

		A	B	C	D
15.	Teachers be trusted with power to operate these sanctions	81	80	56	37
16.	There be right of appeal by pupils against teachers	100	98	90	98
17.	Rules and contracts be clearly spelled out	98	82	63	52
18.	Head teacher have ultimate authority subject to appeal	98	82	61	34
19.	"Prefects" be used for discipline	71	63	42	21
20.	More attention be paid to discipline and authority	92	99	78	56

The most interesting thing about these responses was that pupils and parents (of course, with exceptions) were, as it seemed to us, much more closely in touch with a proper understanding of discipline and authority than were educational theorists – or even, as it appears, than were teachers! In the course of individual discussions, it seemed that these concepts had largely disappeared in educational theory, and been misunderstood; whereas the pupils and parents, who of course had not been much or at all influenced by such theory, retained a sound commonsense understanding.

This research (again, we make no hard-and-fast claims for it) was at least sufficient for us to take seriously the question of just why, psychologically speaking, there seemed to be a good deal of opposition to the properly-understood notions of discipline and authority. There are, of course, different kinds or levels of opposition. We might talk about the legal or conventional structures which inhibit the practice of discipline, or the less formalized norms which govern people's thinking and behavior (the "climates of opinion," "educational fashions," etc.), or the intellectual fallacies and logical misperceptions which dominate our minds, or the basic fantasies and psychic states which must generate these misperceptions. A grander or at least more orthodox research project might treat each of these kinds or levels under a separate heading: professional lawyers or administrators might talk about the legal system governing schools and teachers, a sociologist or social psychologist about the less formal norms and climates, a logician about the fallacies, and a clinical psychiatrist about the fantasies.

While an extension of our work along these lines is much to be hoped for, there is some danger of over-specialization. It is likely to be the case that some one or more very *general* ideas of (in Aristotelian terms) *practical syllogisms* dominate the entire scene and permeate all levels. We need, at least, some non-specialized and jargon-free account of a general kind which will tell us, in simple terms, why we do not do what we can see (in our saner moments) that we ought to do.

To speak very generally, then, and in a sense to offer a conclusion in advance, we might say that the basic problem here is the *toleration of being separate*. Exercising authority and imposing sanctions involve *distancing* oneself from the other person in obvious ways. First, one is acting not as an equal or a friend, but as an impersonal authority and in a sense, therefore, not as a person at all, though one still remains a person when exercising this authority. Second, one is acting contrary to the desires of the other, i.e. preventing him from doing what he wants, perhaps making him suffer (by sanctions or the temporary withdrawal of affection) in fairly clear-cut ways. The problem is to continue valuing oneself when one has, to put it dramatically, made temporary enemies of other people.

One way of solving this problem, now difficult to adopt for liberals in this and many other societies, is to see oneself as in touch with, sharing in some *external* source or sponsor of values. To take an extreme case, if a man sees himself as the prophet of the Lord, or as ordained by the Party to keep the revolution going, he will be able to alienate himself from others because they are, so to speak, not his real spiritual home: his real home is with the Lord or the Party. Victorian parents in their society, at least by repute, kept their nerve in respect to discipline by these means: they felt and believed that they were on the side of the Right, not in the psychically weak sense that they believed in the rationality of what they enforced, but in the much stronger sense that they felt the Right to have some sort of solid existence external to themselves – if not bound up with God, then at least more substantial than the apparently weak notion of "being reasonable."

Suppose now, as seems to be the case with many people, that this feeling is denied us. We would now feel that we have no solid *locus standi* as authorities at all. We could not, as it were, be fathers ourselves, because there would be no solid father with whom we could identify and be at home. The only alternative, as it seems to us, would be that we must all be children: all on the same level, sharing and enjoying things together without the need for rules, regulations, authorities, punishments and the whole apparatus of discipline. For this would seem to offer us an alternative home, a tender-minded environment of "messing in" with our equals, in an atmosphere of *care, concern*, and so forth. The fantasy is one of small children playing happily together, enjoying things for their own sake, being *convivial*. If (we feel) we could really make this work, then we need not be separate: there would be no external powers to join up with, but there would always be our friends, fellow-workers, comrades, chums, mates, etc.

Many contemporary phenomena may be cited as instances of this basic fantasy. We may mention, heterogeneously and in no sort of order, the vast quantity of left-wing or progressivist writing (Illich and others) which stems either from Marxist fears of "alienation" and/or Rousseauesque feelings about the support and friendliness of "nature;" the ethical relativism which has infected even moderately respectable philosophical circles; the extremist phenomena of youth groups (the hippie communes, squats, and so on) which demonstrate the fantasy of infantile sharing in a clear form; the passion for "integration" and "breaking down barriers" – both in terms of distinctions between school subjects and in terms of differences between types of pupils ("mixed ability," etc.) – which itself shows the fear of separation or isolation in any form; and the general fashion for "participation," "democratic consultation," and the like which has overtaken so many institutions in higher education and elsewhere.

One important feature relevant to all this – whether it be best described as an aspect or a consequence of the fear of being separate – is the *absence of trust*. At the level of rationality, it is entirely plain that we have to trust people with authority and power in order to get certain jobs efficiently done, or done at all. The actual delegation of power, however, depends on the existence of some kind of trust, which in turn may be seen as dependent on being able to tolerate filling some place or position in a hierarchy or structured system. This sort of place filling is not only tolerable but positively inviting if, though only if, we accept and feel at home with the criteria by which the places are allotted. If we are not at home with them, we feel isolated and separated. To fill the place, and allow other people to fill their places, is thus ultimately dependent on the tolerance of separation. Either we feel reasonably secure in our separateness, and say things like, "Oh, well, he is the teacher (policeman, expert, etc.) after all," "He's a reliable chap, let him get on with the job," or we do not feel secure, and try to drown our isolation by huddling together in committees, "participating," or trying to get some "general consensus" by constant chatter.

Plato and a long line of later thinkers believed that it was possible and desirable to impose authority from above, and to make such imposition permanently effective. There are at least some doubts about the desirability of this idea. Yet even if it were desirable, the psychic roots of the opposition – if our suggestions are at all near the mark – cast even more doubt on the possibility of implementing it. One might, indeed, imagine a society (one version could resemble Orwell's *1984*) in which authority was successfully imposed by sufficient psychic control; yet the possibility of such a situation remaining permanent is questionable, and for nearly all actual societies as they exist today, it is a matter for academic discussion to even posit such society. This means that the only way forward, especially for our own and similar societies, must be by the achievement of greater *understanding* of discipline and authority, from which comes the emotional and practical acceptance of them.

There are reasons why such understanding and acceptance must *begin*, at least, by greater conceptual clarity. It might be supposed, as an alternative, that "common sense" or "experience" will eventually do the trick; perhaps things will eventually both be and seem so bad to ordinary people that there will be a "swing of the pendulum," a "backlash" in favor of authority. But such swings may be no more than the takeover of one fear by another: the dread of chaos, rather than separation, may take its turn to invade the ego and lead to a different social outlook and other kinds of political structures: an obsessive puritanism, or dictatorships. But greater rationality can only emerge if we *learn* from these swings. Characteristically, neither individuals nor societies "return to common sense" *simply* under the pressure of dramatic events: such pressure is much more likely to drive them further in the direction of the nonsensical and the doctrinaire.

The Moral Manager

To put things fairly bluntly, and without the benefit of more sophisticated sociological or psychoanalytic theory, it is as if most of us still think of authority in the way that members of a very primitive society or very young children might think of it – not as a necessary piece of equipment to get certain things done, but in a semi-magical way (rather as one might believe in "blue blood" or "the divine right of kings"). Many of our respondents were either "in favor of authority," or "against it;" most were perhaps ambivalent toward it. Specifically in reference to the teacher's authority, there was clearly a feeling that teachers either should or should not be – to put it dramatically – invested with some sort of numinous power calling for "respect," if not awe; rather like priests, they were seen either as having this power (and therefore they ought not to be jostled, sworn at, or treated as ordinary human beings), or as pretenders, "no better than we are" (and therefore they ought to be stripped of all power).

However fanciful this may seem, it at least fits the numerous remarks made by interviewees which had no connection with *rational* authority at all – the constant reference to sex, bad language, dress and so forth. We do not say that these features are unimportant if, as may well be the case, they are connected in the *pupils'* minds with the power of teachers; just as, although we know that monarchs excrete, simple-minded people might lose respect for the crown if they actually saw one doing so. Such is the power of fantasy or magic. Rational discipline and authority, of course, depend on understanding the point of *entitlement*, of entrusting certain people with certain delimited powers to do a certain job.

The Psychological Background to Moral Education

This is a matter of rules and adherence to rules, not of being swayed by charisma.

For fairly obvious social reasons, which must presumably include at least the rise in power (together with increased leisure, money and articulateness) of a working class now largely alienated from traditional authorities, and perhaps also the natural decay in acceptance of such authority-sponsoring metaphysics as Christianity, respect for visible holders of authority — for actual teachers, policemen, statesmen, parents, and priests — has declined over the last four or five decades, perhaps for longer. But it has not been replaced by respect for rational authority; that seems to be too sophisticated a concept for the ordinary intelligence to grasp, or rather too impersonal a practice for our feelings to accept wholeheartedly. It is *not* the case that, for instance, respect for the law has increased as respect for judges and policemen has diminished, nor that respect for business contracts has grown as fear of bosses has declined, nor that respect for the impersonal rules required to run schools has become greater as the teacher has come to be held in less awe.

All this may be more or less familiar ground, but it presents a basic problem which may be roughly stated thus: given people as they are – that is, apparently incapable of firmly grasping and using the notion of rational authority – should we (a) try to *educate* them so that they can obtain such a grasp, or (b) give rational authority up as an unachievable goal, and reinforce some kind of non-rational authority? The former move will, or course, naturally appeal to those of a tender-minded and (roughly) "liberal" disposition; the latter, to those who are more tough-minded, and are prepared to see "law and order" flourish at almost any cost. In the wider political field, a broad distinction may be drawn between those who look for salvation in terms of more *democracy, participation, autonomy* and so forth, and those who feel that society's only hope may lie in "a strong man," "a hard line," or even "dictatorship." It is a regrettable symptom of our own intellectual incompetence that the words *discipline* and *authority* have come to be associated – wrongly, as we have seen – almost exclusively with the latter.

The most important point is to see the lunacy of taking sides. Returning to our question, we can see (a) that there must be at least *some* people who have a proper grasp of the concepts, some "educated" class, some set of individuals who will be able to transmit their understanding to others, or insofar as that proves impossible, will be able to make the right judgments on their behalf. So the desirability of more education about discipline is clear enough. But we can also see (b) that even if only in order to be *able to educate* people in discipline, our schools (and indeed our society) must be reasonably trouble-free, that we must have order and obedience in the first place if our "liberal" aims are to be fulfilled. Moreover, there will also always be some people – near-idiots, psychopaths, and so on – who cannot or will not, however hard we try, grasp the necessary concepts; not everything can, in practice, be achieved by education.

Teachers are in a peculiar, indeed, virtually a unique position, for they have the dual role of (a) education, and (b) keeping order. Most other people in positions of authority are concerned only with ensuring that certain things get done, that certain rules are obeyed – it is not their job, or not primarily their job, to *teach* anything to anyone. In the minds of many teachers, it appears, there is a conflict between education and keeping order. It is as if "educating" or "teaching" *means*, for them, something essentially "non-authoritarian," involving only the children's interest, or their willing participation. Hence the term "discipline" comes to stand (wrongly) for something rather sophisticated and remote from the idea of obedience to authority in a task-like situation; it comes to stand, perhaps, for what might be meant by "self-discipline" or even something like "being genuinely absorbed in some activity," or "wanting to learn." (Something of the same role-conflict may perhaps be observed in social workers and others).

But it is entirely clear that *teachers*, at least, *must* be clear about authority, for they are the people who have the task of educating the coming generation in that respect. Whatever may be gained by educating people, to understand and practice rational authority can only be gained via teachers. The obvious first step, then, must be in teacher education. We are not saying here that we should delay other steps perhaps equally obvious (and to be discussed later); by "first" we mean that it has a clear logical priority, that it is a step that we quite evidently *must* take, whatever else we do. Nor, of course, are we saying that we need not bother to educate *other* people, parents, educational administrators, and so on, in this respect, but that the natural priority lies in teacher education. Once teachers themselves have a proper grasp of discipline, they can join academics in considering what else needs to be done.

The Moral Manager

TAKING THE FIRST STEP

What would this first step consist of? Initially we might want to say that teacher education should include more "philosophy," since that subject is concerned with clarifying concepts. That is a correct view, provided that "philosophy" is used in the right way: to refer to a study and a context of communication in which the *meanings* of words are properly understood; no particular partisan "line" is taken about educational or other issues; and the prejudices and fantasies of those taking part are diminished by an increase in their clarity and common sense. All this has to be stressed, because a good deal of what is called *philosophy of education*, particularly concerning the topic of discipline, in fact does not do this job; rather, it simply reinforces or sophisticates certain fantasies. This vice is, of course, common to all of us; we are not here trying to pass arrogant comments on the writing of other authors. Our point is simple: unless "philosophy" *does* give us clarity and diminish our fantasies, it is of no use and may even be harmful.

It follows, then, that the important goal for teacher education is not best achieved by saying that student-teachers should "do more philosophy;" for that, in the eyes of many administrators and others who influence teacher education, might simply mean more man-hours, examinations and books, more professors of the philosophy of education, and more high-minded talk about "the aims of education," "the basis of ethics," "schools and society," and so forth.

It might even be plausible to suggest that student-teachers should do *less* in other areas that might be labeled *sociology*, *psy-*

chology or *educational theory*. The responses of interviewees make it quite clear that what is taught, or at least what comes across, under these headings often reinforces, where it does not actually create, certain recognizable fantasies about, for instance, "the authoritarian teacher," "intrinsic motivation," or "convivial institutions." Very little *educational theory*, indeed, is free of partisan bias. What teachers chiefly need are clearer heads and a stronger nerve. Most *educational theory* is demonstrably rubbish.

This does *not* mean that student teachers should spend less time in *hard thinking* and more time in what some quaintly describe as *practical* training. There is a fashion, stemming perhaps partly from a disenchantment with the usual content of *educational theory*, for laying more stress on this "practical" side; but this in itself will not and cannot help the students to retain and enlarge their common sense and conceptual competence. They need many man-hours of argument and conceptual discussion, in which a tough-minded accuracy about the meanings of words may help to defend them against fantasy and prejudice. Without this, they have little chance of remaining levelheaded in a world of constantly changing educational fashion and pressure.

EDUCATION AND THE MORAL MANAGER

The previous discussion directly applies to the state of the business world, too. The moral manager, his or her employees, and indeed, senior management, are all educated in the same system. In order to understand personal dynamics in the workplace, it helps to understand the educational forces that shape and affect employee reaction to rules, regulations, and the people who uphold them. A knee-jerk reaction to defiance may cause a minor problem to snowball. The history of labor relations is rife with "us versus them" battles that could have been resolved far more quickly if the parties had been able to understand each other's positions and "walk a mile in their shoes."

REFERENCES

Wilson, J. et al. (1968). *Introduction to moral education*. London: Penguin.

_____. (1973). *The assessment of morality*. Slough, U.K.: NFER Publishing Co.

_____. (1977). *Philosophy and practical education*. London: NKP.

_____. (1987). *What philosophy can do*. London: Macmillan.

_____. (1988). *A preface to morality*. London: Macmillan.

Chapter Two
Morals for Managers

Moral management contains certain semantic building blocks. This chapter will help create the foundation for describing the qualities of moral management. We intend to raise (not solve) some basic questions: questions that face anyone who wants to reflect seriously on conducting a certain enterprise. "Moral education for managers" may serve as an initial description of that enterprise. But that itself jumps a number of guns, since the headings we use inevitably carry certain meanings and connotations which already point to different agendas: they suggest different contents, processes and methods, in effect different enterprises. That deserves some discussion in itself. Here are the key points:

One: We have available a number of different words and phrases: *moral education, values education, the transmission of values, professional ethics, business ethics*. We also talk, not always with precision, of *education, indoctrination,* and *training*; and we may even interchange the term *managers* with *executives* or *leaders* or perhaps *decision makers*. The terminology often changes with fashion, and its variety testifies to the important fact that we are far from clear about the (perhaps significantly different) concerns that we have in mind under these headings. Thus, in the U.K. there is a well-entrenched program for pupils in secondary schools called *Personal and Social Education*, but nobody is clear about what it means — does it include *moral education* (whatever *that* means)? In the U.S.A. and elsewhere *values education* is a popular phrase, but that too is unclear, if only because it is unclear what sort of values we have in mind (presumably not property or real estate values, or the values of x and y in mathematical equations). What in practice goes on under these titles becomes entrenched and, as it were, self-sealed; there is, for instance, a recognized set of topics dealt with under *business ethics*. But it is in fact a very open question what the agenda of *business ethics* ought to be, what *business ethics* is really *about*.

2. So we ought to consider what *moral education* is about, what it is to be a *manager* or to *manage* something (I talk of *managing* my finances, my horse; my husband: are these cases of *management* in the required sense?), or what *moral education for managers* could actually mean. That question would have to be answered before we could get down to any empirical work on how such education could actually be done, otherwise we should not know just what we were trying to do in the first place. It is not just a matter of linguistic pre-

cision or pedantry, but of describing our concerns clearly and appropriately. Without that there may be not only confusion but disaster. If we consider, for example, the Hitler Youth Camps, which aimed at controlling the character and values of young people in accordance with Nazi doctrine, whether or not we are prepared to call that *moral education* has pragmatic and not just terminological importance.

3. We have, rightly, the idea that people occupy/fulfill certain roles (as managers, or policeman, or soldiers, or whatever), and that whatever we mean by *morality* or *ethics* must surely have some connection with these roles. Suppose we were to talk of moral education for mothers or mistresses, magistrates or ministers of the church, morticians, and matadors. Then not only would different moral considerations be relevant to these different roles, but they would be relevant in different ways. And in some cases we might wonder whether *role* was really the right word to use: it is not clear that being a good mother, for instance, consists primarily of anything we should want to call *playing a role*. Similarly, it is not clear whether or in what sense I should *manage* my wife or husband, rather than just relating to and communicating with her/him in a certain way. These examples make it clear that it is important to define the terms *manager* or *management*, and to distinguish them from any other kinds of influence or relationship. Do officers who lead their troops into battle *manage* them, do religious evangelists *manage*

their congregations, and do close friends or lovers *manage* each other in any sense at all? If we conceive of *managers* as occupying a certain role, we have to be alert about just what the role is and what *management* as a concept logically includes (and, just as important, what it excludes).

4. The concepts *moral* and *ethical* present even more difficult problems. To pick out some of the most salient ones:

(a) We have to decide whether to base our moral education on a particular moral *content*, or to aim rather at giving our clients certain items of mental *equipment* whereby they are to make up their own minds about moral issues. The former (and more popular) procedure raises questions about the source from which we are to derive any such content—our own moral intuitions? The values of the western world? Some kind of social or international consensus? And about what we are to do if (as will certainly happen) some of our clients challenge that content—do we just tell them to shut up? I have argued for providing mental tools that enable people to analyze and decide moral questions for themselves, but a clear decision has to be made one way or the other.

(b) We have to decide whether *moral* is to include only what might be called social or interpersonal morality, where other people's interests are affected, or whether to include also personal ideals and what philosophers have called *self-regarding* (as opposed to *other-regarding*) virtues. Even on a desert island, I can be lazy, or greedy, or cowardly, or imprudent, though I can hardly be unjust or dishonest: I still have a moral or ethical character which can be praised or blamed. Is the moral education of managers to include this aspect of morality? And if we restrict it to the interests of others, is the term *others* to include only human beings or also animals, and can perhaps *the environment* be viewed as important in its own right rather than just for the benefit of human beings?

(c) Even more important, what is to count as a *moral* (as opposed to a non-moral) quality? As a manager, I may be unjust or dishonest: these are clearly moral qualities. I may also be handsome or athletic or clever, and these are not normally counted as *moral qualities*. But I may also be by nature spontaneous or cautious, outgoing or withdrawn, severe or easy-going, prudent or carefree, blind or insightful, with or without a sense of humor. These qualities are certainly part of my character and my personality; they may or may not be under the control of my will, and some of them at least will be relevant to my merits as a manager. But which of them do we take on board as *moral*? If we have a program of moral education for mangers, just what qualities do we address and attempt to engender under the heading?

5. The question arises of how culture-free or time-free our moral education for managers is to be, or, we might say, how parochial or generalized it is to be. We bump up against that question in (at least) two ways:

(a) Do we think that across-the-board generalizations can

be made about *management* quite independently of *what* is to be managed (a sweetshop, General Motors, a school, a prison, a love affair)? And even if we do, does it follow that the same *moral* issues and qualities are relevant to all cases? It would be nice if we could produce a program that was valid for all institutions in all cultures. But that may be utopian, so we shall have to delimit the scope of our program with some care ("a program for managers of middle-sized corporations in the western world," or whatever).

(b) Certain social (cultural, legal) facts will in any case be relevant, because they constitute the parameters within which managers have to work. Thus, there may be generalizations to be made, and moral lessons to be learned about managing any kind of army or any kind of money-lending organization. But it makes a difference that Julius Caesar could decimate his troops (after which nine surviving soldiers fought better then the original ten), and that Cicero could lend money at 60% interest, privileges now denied to most generals and usurers.

6. As these examples may suggest, there is a question about how far the role of a manager (whatever exactly that may be) in this or that society is itself morally viable. Usury was long counted as a sin within Christian cultures, and the paid-up pacifist will have no interest in the moral education of generals. Any manager who is morally educated, as such will have to believe that the enterprise he manages is morally desirable, or at least morally harmless. In the case of

business management, conducted (roughly) according to the principles of capitalist economics at least in most western countries, that is perhaps not very hard to believe. There are not other serious candidates or rival theories for the production of wealth and high standard of living, and dissatisfaction with it predictably takes the form of amorphous protest rather than the offering of any rational alternative. But managers and others who participate in this enterprise must be clear about why it is desirable from a moral viewpoint; otherwise they cede the moral high ground to the protesters. There are indeed moral questions about the price to be paid for unrestrained laissez-faire, and the comparative weight we should attach to wealth as against other human goods. Nobody (in his right mind) wishes to replace capitalism by Marxism. But there are various forms of capitalism, not all of which are of equal moral worth. And there are various products of capitalism of which the same is true (we need think only of tobacco and other drugs, and I might even question whether I really need seventy-two different kinds of breakfast cereal to choose among in the supermarket). The managers of various businesses need to believe that the product they sell, not just capitalism in general, actually meets human needs.

7. This relates to point number four above, the question of what we count as *moral* or *ethical*. In the western world, at least, we inherit a particular conception of morality, what Bernard Williams (1985) describes as

"morality: the peculiar institution," closely connected with a certain kind of guilt and with certain contents (not least with sexual morality). It is a post-Christian, or at least a post-Kantian and post-Lutheran conception, and it should not be swallowed whole. As a result of this inheritance, when we talk of *immoral* or still more of *unethical* behavior, or of *business ethics* or *professional ethics*, we have chiefly in mind the somewhat Pharisaic idea of keeping our moral hands clean. The intent guiding our behavior is to avoid giving offense, or landing in the magistrate's court, or in the gossip columns of newspapers. It is a profoundly negative conception of morality; as if, so long as we refrained from doing (or be detected in doing) X or Y or Z, we could count ourselves as *moral*. That conception must at least be seen as one-sided; morality must surely include something more positive, and the content of moral education for managers more than (though not less than) the avoidance of vice or corruption. We cannot consider that, for example, if I sell a desirable product, if I manage my workforce efficiently with genuine concern for their welfare, and if in general I display the positive moral qualities necessary for these ends, I may reasonably be forgiven if my sexual behavior is not all that it should be or even if I sometimes dip my hand into the till. Any respectable morality must consist primarily of doing good and having those virtues that enable me to do good, rather than just avoiding scandal, which makes it all the more necessary to identify those virtues that enable me to do good, rather than just avoiding scandal, which makes it all the more necessary to identify those virtues. *Professional ethics* should be more concerned with these virtues than with just making sure that the professional's hands are clean; just as the Hippocratic oath in medicine involves a positive commitment to cure, and not just the injunction to avoid seducing one's patients.

8. There is a problem about how far we conceive moral education for managers as applying to them just *qua* managers, or as applying to them more widely *qua* people. It is, perhaps regrettably, true that a person's moral behavior may be admirable in particular roles, but disastrous outside them. We are amazed that at least some Nazis were good husbands and fathers, kind to animals, conscientious and efficient, determined and courageous in battle, but so they were. To what extent can I be a good manager without also being a good person? The answer to this is not at all clear, and obviously it will turn partly on the question raised in number three above, the question of what is involved in the concept marked *management*. Questions of this sort depend very much on the words we use; for instance, we may ask whether one can be a good teacher without being a good person (or at least having certain moral virtues). But the answer may differ depending on whether the word *teacher* is to mean just a *formal instructor* or perhaps something wider, and the term *educator* to be used for someone from whom people may learn (by example or a certain kind of relationship, not just formal instruction). Use of notions like *efficiency* does not help,

because efficiency is relative to certain ends or goals or values: I can be, in one sense, an efficient school principal without being a good one. We recognize this with some roles (if indeed *role* is an appropriate term here): we do not normally even talk of *efficient* wives or husbands, or parents or friends, because we appreciate that the goods that such people produce are more impalpable. How far that consideration applies to managers is an open question.

These are, as I have said, only some of the questions that arise when we start to think about morality and management. They are essentially questions about our concepts or conceptions; and they are very far from *academic* in any pejorative sense, for the obvious reason that our conceptions drive our practice. How we see *management* or *morality*, what we mean by those terms, and the way in which we connect them, will profoundly affect what we actually do, just as our conceptions of love and marriage shape our behavior in personal relationships.

It does not follow that we should hold our horses until all such questions have been answered, partly because there is an urgent need for making a pragmatic connection between morality and management in the form of some educational program, but also because some of the answers may become clearer as we proceed in practice, by trial and error. There will of course be many empirical facts relevant to such programs; I have not been here concerned with these, if only because just *what* empirical facts are relevant will depend on our initial conceptions. But this too may become clearer *en courant*, in the course of actually operating the programs and trying to assess them; sitting in an armchair and reflecting is but one way of achieving conceptual clarity.

Nevertheless, we need to keep the questions constantly in mind, and monitor our practice in the light of them. If we fail to do that, our practice becomes self-sealed and immune to any basic criticism; it may even fail to address any legitimate or important concern at all, or it may address the wrong kind of concerns (like the Hitler Youth camps). In this way, we take our own conceptions for granted, and impose them uncritically on our clients; this lacks intellectual credibility, and may well be regarded as unjust or even immoral. But there are also severe practical consequences: we shall do no more than add to the plethora of *initiatives* which now go on under headings like *moral education*, initiatives whose titles and content constantly change, and which come into and go out of fashion. The lack of a solid conceptual foundation brings the whole enterprise into disrepute.

We have suggested, if only by implication, that the kind of reflection we need consists of clarifying our concepts and the meanings of the words we use, and we have tried to show something of the importance of this for our practice. This exercise involves a certain kind of procedure, which may be called *philosophical*, and has obvious connections with certain brands or styles of philosophy (*linguistic philosophy* or *conceptual analysis*). We want to underline the importance of this kind of reflection (whether or not we call it *philosophy* and whether or not we make this connection), because almost any other kind of philosophy—any theory, or doctrine, or school of thought, or ideology—will itself involve imposing a certain conception on the enterprise of moral education. But just such conceptions need our inspection and criticism. It is a piecemeal process; we have to take seriously whatever concepts we actually bump up against (*management*, *morality*, and so on) and get clear about them, before attempting any kind of overall *philosophy of management* or *moral theory*. This general point of procedure (or method, or heuristics) is perhaps more important than any of the specific points I have mentioned above. We must not expect philosophers to produce an overall, large-scale *theory* that will solve these problems for us: we have to do this work for ourselves.

However, certain fairly general questions do arise which are dealt with in that branch of inquiry that we call *moral philosophy* or *ethics*, and some of these questions cannot be avoided. The specific questions in number one through eight above are really questions of classification, or taxonomy, or categorization. They are not themselves moral or ethical questions; they are about what we should count or classify as *management*, *moral*, etc., about producing a viable conceptual framework for a program of moral education for managers. But even if we succeed in doing this, we still have the task of determining how managers should operate within that framework, and what kind of rationale they should have for their moral decision making. We mean this: to educate people in (for instance) science, or mathematics, or history, we obviously first need to establish these clear categories, to know what to count as *science* or *history*, and distinguish them from superstition or myth. But in addition to this, or perhaps while actually doing it, we also need to establish *how to perform* in these areas — in particular, what counts as a *good reason*, or a relevant consideration, or a sound argument, in science or history. We teach children *how* to think (not necessarily *what* to think) in each area or form of thought. The same must be true of education in morality.

That is an obvious point, but commonly neglected. We tend not to see *morality* as a form of thought with its own reasons and relevant considerations, in the way that we see science or history or other forms of thought. But it is seen as a "brute" social phenomenon for which different individuals and cultures may have different rationales or even no rationale at all. It may be thought to include a very wide variety of items, not just being unjust or dishonest or cowardly, but appearing unveiled in public, if one is a woman, or eating pork, or going to bed with people of the same sex, or committing hara-kiri if one has failed in one's duty. The point here is not just that the content of each individual's morality varies, that they have different *values*; that in itself would be unobjectionable (after all, different scientists and historians have different scientific and historical beliefs). It is rather that these different items seem to come from quite different sources, and to be justified (if they are justified at all) by quite different sorts of reasons. Some values, like justice and honesty, seem to have some kind of *utilitarian* basis: justice and honesty are necessary if we are to do business successfully with each other or run any kind of coherent society. Values of this kind—truth, justice, honesty, respect, compassion, duty, responsibility – appear in one form or another in many of the world's religious teachings, and figure prominently in moral teachings of many groups; among the welter of *moral principles*, these may be considered to be universally recognized as moral virtues. But other items seem more like aesthetic judgments or taboos, and have more to do with what we find disgusting or repellent or obscene, whilst others again seem concerned with preserving our dignity or honor or ego ideal ("samurai never surrender," "gunfighters never back down from the draw," "big boys don't cry"). It is a very mixed bag; and this alone may make it hard to know even how to classify beliefs or behavior as *moral* rather than non-moral (see number four above). More important, it will not be clear just what kind of reasons should be operative in this form of thought or department of life.

There are good tactical reasons for counting as *moral* any principles or ideals or behavior patterns which are overriding in a person's behavior (as considerations of social etiquette, for instance, are not overriding), irrespective of their contents. This approach has the important advantage that nobody is excluded from a program of moral education, because everyone (on his account) will have *some* overriding principles that dictate his behavior, whatever the contents of those principles may be. I follow Hare (1981) in preferring this criterion of classification, and also in acknowledging the supreme importance of the Golden Rule or principle of universalisability. Roughly, this rule states that I must be prepared to universalize my moral principles, so that I accept the legitimacy of other people treating me as I treat them, and count them as equals: I am not the only pebble on the beach. This rule may indeed carry us a long way; the question "How would *you* like it if *you* were assaulted/ lied to/ stolen from?" has considerable force. But it does not carry us all the way, if only because morality may reasonably be thought to extend beyond social or interpersonal morality, that is, beyond considerations of justice and into the more murky area where various ideals, taboos, feelings of shame or repulsion, honor or aesthetic appropriateness, do in fact dictate a great deal of human behavior.

The matter is still philosophically controversial (compare Hare 1981 with Williams 1985, for instance — and the philosophical debate continues), and it may be that the question "what counts as a good moral reason?" has to be left open for managers (or anybody else) to decide for themselves. At some points we may be tempted to throw in the towel, and say, as an example, that for people in Islamic cultures there are good reasons for enforcing the strict dress code of *sharia* for women; to say that for certain kinds of Christians there are good reasons for thinking homosexuality wicked; for certain kinds of Hindus there are good reasons for not eating beef, and so on — that there are, at least in these cases, no "objectively" good or universal reasons at all upon which to base moral decisions. But this idea opens the door for anyone who has sufficiently strong feelings about something to make a morality out of those feelings: to think, for instance, that Jews should be persecuted, or women forcibly circumcised. Even in the teeth of the Golden Rule, someone may cling to this morality, even if he/she was, or imagined him/herself to be, a Jew or a woman. Before accepting this idea, we should reflect further.

The Moral Manager

There is one way forward from this apparent impasse, which consists in reflecting on what is to count as (any kind of) *reasoning* at all. Characteristically, a great deal of our behavior consists of brute emotional reactions unmediated by reason. We look upon certain foodstuffs, or sexual behavior, or other objects and appearances, and react to them almost instinctively; we entertain a picture of ourselves, our honor of dignity, and act it out without thought. Thus the fundamental objection to racism, for instance, is not that it is based on a set of well-considered reasons that happen to be inconsistent with our own. Rather, racism is not really based on any serious reasoning at all (though of course racists may propound various *post hoc* rationalizations, like Hitler's rationalization about the Jews); it is more like some kind of nonrational *allergy* than it is like some feature of a coherent moral view. It is not clear that what are given as reasons—"Because he's black," "Because she's a woman," "Because eating pork is forbidden," "Because it offends my honor," "Because it's just disgusting"— are really *reasons*, in the sense that they may only explain our attitudes and behavior, but they do not justify our attitudes and behavior. And the same holds for other rationalizations commonly offered as reasons: "Because all my friends do," "Because some authority says so," and even "Because it's socially inappropriate."

Some of these may be, or may be turned into, genuine reasons or justifications by being connected with recognizable goods or interests. Even "Because he's black" may count as a reason if we are distributing suntan lotion or (perhaps) casting *Othello*; and what authorities forbid, or what is socially inappropriate, may justify what we do (we do not want to break the law or upset our neighbors). But the test is whether, in our minds, our reasons are in fact connected with these goods or interests or whether we are simply expressing and acting out our own feelings and taking those feelings as somehow self-authenticating. I may be disgusted by something, but that in itself does not show that it is really disgusting. The difference is crucial: either we are genuinely concerned to promote some good or avoid some evil, in which case we have to assure ourselves by some process of reason that it really is a good or an evil, or else we are concerned simply to reinforce our feelings. Of course, we all have such feelings, and we have to live with them; we may even make moral principles out of them in the sense that they often overridingly govern our behavior. But that does not show that the principles are in any sense rational or reasonable.

Reasoning and Morality

We believe that in any program of moral education recognition of this distinction would cut a good deal of ice. We need not dictate to our clients any specific moral content, or even any particular set of reasons. But we can legitimately demand of them that they engage in reasoning rather than in just acting out their feelings and, as it were, pretending to themselves as well as to other people that they have a basis in reason. When that demand is made in discussion and dialogue, wherein individuals are called upon to justify their moral beliefs and defend them against criticism, the effect may be profound; at least they come to see that their feelings are not self-validating. The sharing involved in such dialogue is crucial: we gain ground in that we are not simply dictating moral content, but rather are encouraging mutual reflection.

In that light, the context of any program for moral education may be more important than the content. Those who devise or administer such programs ought, for certain, to reflect in advance on the questions raised above. But it is unlikely that even those questions will be answered except in a context of small-group discussion where individuals trust each other enough to share them, let alone more practical questions of moral behavior which also have to be faced. It cannot be done *de haut en bas*, by mass lecture or the reading of prescribed literature. Almost everything turns on whether we can engender a serious desire to get clear, to make sense, to share meaning, and to submit willingly to the discipline of reason in general; and that is primarily a matter of establishing a context which will promote and sustain such a desire. This is a task for psychologists rather than for philosophers.

To summarize, we have suggested:

1. In point A above, that there are a number of basic conceptual questions which need to be considered before formulating any program of moral education for managers; these questions are primarily to be addressed by those who devise such programs.
2. In point B above, that we need to reflect on the whole business of moral reasoning, without which we can hardly educate anyone in morality at all, and that

moral reasoning must be applied to ethical questions by anyone involved in any such program;
3. As a brief postscript, that we should pay attention to the educational context in which these and other questions are considered and discussed. All that may appear as a somewhat daunting task. But if moral education for managers is to be a coherent and ongoing enterprise, rather than a mere fashion (or perhaps a kind of conscience money), it is a task that we have to address. The enterprise is too important for us to skimp on it: we have to base it on permanent and secure foundations.

REFERENCES

Hare, R.M. (1981). *Moral thinking*. Oxford: University Press.

Williams, B. (1985). *Ethics and the limits of philosophy*. London: Fontana.

Wilson, J. (1987). A *preface to morality*. London: Macmillan.

————. (1990). A *new introduction to moral education*. London: Cassel.

Chapter Three
Morality, Management, and Passion

There is something curiously absent from any program of moral education or management training, something which can be called "passion." We shall first try to clarify the concept marked by that word, looking at some of the ways in which we describe the aims of moral education and at what these descriptions seem to miss out, and then to relate this to the particular case of moral education for managers.

Characteristically moral educators require of their clients that they should be "caring" or "concerned for others," that they should "treat other people as equals," and not be "selfish." They should adopt "a mature attitude," and have "a sense of responsibility"; perhaps that they should be concerned with "human rights," or "world peace," or "the environment." The emphasis is on kindness, altruism, self-control, sympathy, and an elementary sense of justice; and the general tone is both tender-minded, as when we talk of *caring*, and high-minded, as when we talk of *spiritual education*. That holds even for comparatively sophisticated accounts of the aims of moral education: for instance, Kohlberg's stages of moral development (Kohlberg 1963), or my own account of what the morally educated person requires by way of equipment (Wilson 1990). These lay out certain types of reasoning, general principles, competencies and skills: there is no mention of "passion" or anything like it.

We find the same situation when we turn to moral philosophers. Deontologists talk of "duty" or "obligation," teleologists and utilitarians of "desirable states of affairs"; currently we have "justice ethics" and "caring ethics" and "virtue ethics," but passion plays little or no part in any of these. Even philosophers have to face this fact: that our actions spring from our wants and desires, and some philosophers face this fact squarely (e.g. Williams 1985); but characteristically these wants and desires are simply taken for granted and then subjected to some kind of logical control. Thus, Hare (1981) is concerned with how people handle their overriding desires and preferences; in particular with whether they are willing to "universalize" them (which gives reason a foothold in morality). He does not consider those desires in their own right; they are for him just subject matter. And in any case, not all desires are passions. To obtain any serious account or advocacy of passion we have to go back to Nietzsche, or, in a different vein, to Plato's *Symposium*.

Much of moral philosophy may fairly be described as mealy-mouthed, unduly ironic, in the modern parlance, "wet" or "wimpish;" it is not the sort of thing that is going to appeal to any reasonably red-blooded and healthy adolescent. It is as if we were telling our clients to be "good boys/girls," with the implicit understanding that they are to be trouble-free, self-controlled, tolerably unselfish and (in a certain sense) "reasonable." Our picture of the inner self and its passions seems to be a picture of something essentially dangerous or destructive, something that has to be replaced by a set of more tender-minded feelings, or at least controlled by reason and will power. And of course there is something in this; nobody thinks that we can lead morally good lives, or even self-gratifying lives, simply by acting out our passions without any kind of reflection or control.

Nevertheless, we maintain a negative image of passion, which contrasts interestingly with what we think about it in contexts where we feel that passion is safe, in some way bounded or licensed. For many of us, the arts are separated from our everyday lives and concerns, so they become an obvious example of this phenomenon. Take away passion from the composition, performance, and appreciation of music, for instance, and we are not left with much worth having; so too with drama and poetry. The appreciation of nature seems similarly safe: we do not feel alarmed when Wordsworth says that "the sounding cataract/Haunted me like a passion," we may even envy such feelings. Our admiration extends to the passion of Wittgenstein for philosophy, or Einstein for physics, or to the passion of those who promote some worthy cause, like the abolition of slavery. When it comes to personal relationships, we're less certain. The passion that a mother feels for her children is acceptable, perhaps because it goes along with caring and tenderness. The passionate friendship of David and Jonathan, or Achilles and Patroclus — well, perhaps. But erotic passion between adults, of the same kind as that depicted between Romeo and Juliet or Antony and Cleopatra or Anna Karenina and Vronsky — no, that is too dangerous to countenance. As a society, we feel that kind of passion needs to be experienced secondhand, in the works of art that depict it.

These examples may help us toward a somewhat clearer account of passion. We are speaking of passion as something that overcomes us, something that in a sense we suffer from (Latin *patior*, Greek *pashco*), rather than something that we choose and entirely control; it is something which we are driven or overwhelmed by. Passion has a compulsive quality. It was not that Wittgenstein was *interested* in philosophy, or *cared for* it or even thought it important; rather he felt a compulsion to engage in it. Unsurprisingly, this engenders alarm in a person, just because it is not generated by will and judgment, not by *voulu*. It is also pleasurable, because it brings into play parts of the self that we were previously unaware of in ourselves; passion gives our lives more depth and meaning.

That is what I think makes passion so intense and disturbing, neither calm nor judicious, a mixture of pleasure and pain. I am in a sense addicted, drawn like a moth to the light, because I lack something that only the object of my passion can give me. It is an active desire, a strong movement of the heart and the senses toward the object. The object is attractive or magnetic; it has an inherent beauty or magic power in it that overwhelms me and draws me to it; I seek it out and I am not happy until I possess it or engage closely with it. That holds not only for erotic passion in the strict sense, but for any genuine passion: there is something about philosophical problems, foreign languages, or surfing that I cannot resist; it is not something that I am happy to take or leave alone. The experience is often almost sensual — I am in love with these things; I do not just love them.

Why should that particular kind of desire, or love, or experience be important?

Why should we not be content with what may be equally strong but calmer forms of love or desire, for instance, with affection or cherishing? The answer is that there are some deep parts of the self that can only be elicited in this way, by allowing the self to be vulnerable to this kind of desire. We are right to see passion as dangerous; but the reverse side of that coin is that it brings to consciousness certain needs and feelings which would otherwise lie dormant. When we fall in love, the world changes for us as it does not change if (however desirable that may be) we come to love something or somebody by a mixture of familiarity and judicious attention. In love, we are, so to speak, *shaken up*; and only such shaking can release the relevant feelings.

That is of course because many of such feelings are, quite rightly, repressed or suppressed, for the most part in early childhood. We do not really need Freud to tell us that we cannot allow children to act out all their aggressive and erotic feelings, in their own interests as well as in the interests of other people. But the inevitable result of this is that the adult psyche takes on a certain structure; it becomes more rigid and less plastic; certain feelings are either seen as taboo or banished from consciousness altogether. They are recovered and re-experienced, only when we are taken unaware, as when we fall in love, or as when a piece of music suddenly ravishes us. As Browning put it, "Just when we're safest, there's a sunset-touch: A chorus ending from Euripides...." – and a whole new world of feeling opens up and shatters our complacency.

Passion has often been defended, by romantics and existentialists, simply on the grounds that these experiences are desirable in themselves. They keep us in touch with our basic natures and enable us to see through the kind of sham which we often make of our lives, as Ivan Ilyitch (in Tolstoy's *Death of Ivan Ilyitch*) on his deathbed saw through the sham and hypocrisy of his own life. This argument has merits, but it has the defect of leaving us in the air, so to speak, with experiences: their mere intensity (which may indeed be as much painful as pleasurable) does not help us to structure our lives more satisfactorily. It is a more important point that passion is always a passion *for* something or someone, that passion has a goal and propels us toward the object of our passion, and often toward a new kind of life. The mere *experience* of falling in love may, on a certain view of human life, be seen as desirable, even in a sense educational. But it is more relevant that falling in love propels us toward some form of life in which that passion is gratified, for instance, toward a happy marriage.

So passion must be seen not just as a kind of episodic desire, however intense, but more as incorporating a kind of vision that we are impelled to pursue. Passion is as inimical to impulsive hedonism as it is to an impoverished puritanism. It is at least to some extent durable and geared to non-trivial targets; we distinguish passion from itches or yens or sudden urges and impulses. To have a passion for something or someone is already to have some kind of *commitment*, however vague or unformulated. Passion drives us to action, not just to *experience*.

Let us compare passion with the Christian virtue of *agape*. In one form or another, it is nearest that most programs of moral education get to a positive ideal. But *agape* is not a passion; it is a certain kind of overall virtue or disposition which may trade off various feelings (like the compassion felt by the Good Samaritan), but is itself supposed to be under the control of the will and the judgement, like other virtues. When *agape* turns into a passion, it is directed toward some particular target, i.e., I feel passionate about abolishing slavery, or about ensuring the happiness of my wife or my children, or about the treatment of animals. It is not possible to be passionate about humanity in general, even though it is possible to have the general virtue or disposition of *agape*. Passions cannot be generalized: I may feel erotic passion toward this or that person, but the idea of feeling erotic passion toward everyone is incoherent. Objects of passion have to be, for instance, *my* wife, *my* child, *my* country, *my* political cause, not just any woman or child or country or cause.

So, in general, virtues of justice and benevolence, important though they are, do not touch passion at all. Passion is not conceived as a desideratum for the morally educated person. For along with our picture of our dangerous inner self (and some of its features, particularly eroticism and aggression), we maintain also an impoverished picture of *morality* as a device primarily concerned with suppressing and controlling passion, or shaping passion into a non-destructive force. From this perspective, passion is not a moral virtue. And yet, with a wider conception of morality (perhaps something like "the general ecology of the mind/heart/soul;" see Wilson 1987), it might appear as such. After all, without some element of passion, how much of real value remains in my marriage, my work, my parenting, my creativity, even my hobbies? Of course something remains—my marriage may be safe and comforting, my work useful and not always tedious, my children respectfully brought up, and my leisure pursuits may keep me pleasurably occupied; that is not to be sneezed at. But without passion, I am clearly impoverished, and I may even begin to wonder whether there is any point in being married, or whether my efforts to solve philosophical problems are really worth the trouble. I need something to drive and motivate me, something that goes beyond my will and judgment and even beyond my sense of duty: something which engages me at a level deeper than any of these, something which is more like *eros* than any other kind of love.

In that sense, passion has a certain kind of primacy. Consider again the *overriding desires*, which for Hare (1981) form the basic material of morality and have to be subjected to reason. Of course everyone has some desires or preferences; that is in the nature of human beings. But there are many people, who may have no very *strong* desires or *passion* at all. They are perhaps in a state of depression or anxiety, or perhaps they simply live by rote from day to day, or even hour to hour,

Morality, Management, and Passion

almost like automata, carrying out their duties, but without passion or even much desire. In their lives, there is nothing for morality to be *about*. The rational principles of morality have a purpose: they are designed to maximize human happiness by gratifying human desires in accordance with reason; but if the desires are absent or minimal, the principles have no bite or purchase. Without overriding desires and passions, we might indeed be trouble-free (though we shall not make much of a contribution to life), but it is equally true that morality would have little grip on us. Because to get off the ground, we have to start with a certain capital, the capital of desire and passion; only then can we consider how best to spend or invest it. Without the capital of passion, we can do no serious business at all.

It could be argued that, though passion is important, it lies outside the scope of education, except the kind of education that is devoted to controlling it or giving it an appropriate shape. Educators (it might be thought) can encourage people to express their eroticism in an appropriate context (marriage rather than rape) or their aggression in non-destructive forms (competitive games rather than war); but they cannot teach people to fall in love or to be forceful. But these statements are at best only half-truths. Children are naturally passionate, and the attitude of parents and other educators toward passion in general—whether they themselves admit to and display passion, for instance—makes an enormous difference to the child's ability to retain passion in later life. The educator can guide the child toward activities and forms of life that may engage his passions so that he may find passion in music or game-playing, or nature, or some intellectual pursuit. The educator can, as it were, keep passion alive in the child's mind, or cripple it, or even extinguish it; and that is done as much or more by example and by sharing passion with the child as by any direct teaching or instruction. Sharing passion has nothing to do with *free expression* or just letting the child act out his own impulses without restraint or discipline; it has rather to do with offering the child forms of life in which his passions can find a place.

EDUCATING FOR PASSION

We see that the educator's task is not merely (though of course he has to do this) to repress or suppress the child's unruly or dangerous passions, but also to keep passion alive in the child's heart and mind whilst at the same time offering him forms of life in which it can be safely expressed and gratified. With some kinds of passion, we can see how this may be done, even though much of what we do may be a matter of hit-and-miss, or trial and error. We engage the child in certain activities—games, music, and certain kinds of intellectual enquiry—and hope that they elicit his passion. We do not know enough psychology to identify just what forms of life will elicit passion in what types of children, but at least we can try. We may even have some idea of how to give a shape to the child's aggression, what William James describes as "the moral equivalent of war," so as to avoid actual wars; we can construct rule-governed contexts in which the aggression is not actually damaging. With other types of passion we are more at a loss: we really have no idea how to deal with the erotic passions of children and adolescents. That is the reason that what goes on under the heading of *sex education* seems

Morality, Management, and Passion

too often to miss the mark; it is a mixture of elementary biology and vague moralizing. A great deal of work needs to be done here, but it will not be done at all if we retain an image of passion as dangerous in itself. In truth, our attitude toward passion is deeply irresponsible. On the one hand, we talk of *caring* and *concern for others*; we try to engender feelings of compassion and kindness, to protect the environment and succor the weak. On the other hand, innumerable horrors and disasters surround us: rape, war, murder, racial and other persecution, and cruelty to animals, slavery, and tyranny. These will not be put right by the promotion of moral ideals in a narrow sense of the word *moral* or by religious ideals either; nominal adherence to Christianity, or Buddhism, or Islam, or Judaism, or any other religion offers no defense against these disasters. The only way forward is to accept the primacy of passion and get down to the task of understanding it more fully, within ourselves as well as in other people. We might then be on the way to making moral education more than the promotion of a set of well-meaning platitudes. We could then be in a position to apply the rational principles of morality so that we can gratify our passions in accordance with reason.

MANAGING WITH PASSION

In general it is unsurprising that our impoverished picture of morality profoundly affects our thought and practice, when we consider the moral education of managers, and indeed the whole enterprise of management itself. Consider how most business is conducted: Because we do not see the enterprise of management as itself a moral enterprise, for

The Moral Manager

which particular moral virtues are required and which may be subject to particular moral vices, we relegate it to the category of activities that are morally neutral. It can then be conducted efficiently or inefficiently, competently or incompetently, perhaps wisely or unwisely, but not morally or immorally. Then, if we insist on bringing the idea of morality into management, we can bring it in only *ad hoc* or extrinsically, as it were by the scruff of its neck. We cast around for something (anything) that might be called *moral* or *ethical* in management, and come up with the idea that managers must be *caring* or *concerned* with their workforce, or that there are certain principles of *business ethics* to which they must attend. Morality is thus seen as essentially peripheral to management and not intrinsic to it.

We can see what is wrong with this concept if we consider the management of institutions, which it is easier to perceive as having some kind of moral point or purpose, as, for instance, a school. Suppose one is the principal or headmaster of an independent school, like the famous Dr. Arnold of Rugby School. Then, of course, one has to manage (organize, control, administer) the school efficiently and competently; one may even have to show a profit, or think up ways of making more money in order to extend and improve the school's activities. But one does not separate one's management of the school from one's morality; one does not say, "Right, I am managing my school efficiently— now, how can I inject some morality into it? Ah, yes, I must make sure that none of my teachers does anything morally scandalous, so perhaps I should run up a code of *professional ethics*. I must persuade the

Morality, Management, and Passion

governors to give some of our profits to a worthy charity, and yes, not all the teachers should be upper-class white males. We must make room for women and for other ethnic groups; and of course the school's publicity should show that it provides a useful public service." One's moral virtues and principles and behavior are *part of* one's *management*: it matters what sort of person one is, what sort of vision and ideals one has for the school, how much enthusiasm and passion one puts into one's job as headmaster. It is that which made Thomas Arnold famous, and it is unlikely that he would see himself primarily as a *manager* or even a *leader*, rather than in the role of an inspirer, or a teacher, or even a kind of father.

Not only schools and other educational institutions have moral purpose: there are also churches, prisons, hospitals, charities, social work agencies, and many others. We tend to make a false dichotomy between these institutions: on the one hand, a profit-making organization, on the other, a not-for-profit organization; as if we thought that, just because businesses have to show a profit, they were either subject to a different kind of morality or else to no kind of morality at all. We expect the moral qualities of teachers, priests, doctors, social workers, and even prison warders to infuse their work and their institutions in a way in which we do not expect the moral qualities of bank managers or automobile manufacturers to infuse theirs. But these latter institutions are just as important, just as morally valuable as the former; we could not get far without banks or even without automobiles. We have the false idea that the *profit motive* is in itself inimical to morality; but even churches have to show a profit, and conversely even the most profitable business may offer a public service which is in its own way just as valuable as those offered by a church.

It is here that the idea of passion has to be brought into play. For instance, if one is to be a good merchant banker, it will not be enough to just stay within the law, sponsor a few worthy causes, and adhere to whatever *professional ethics* may apply to merchant banking. One must be passionately concerned to bring benefits to the work by capitalizing appropriate business ventures; and that passion will lead to identifying which ventures are likely to be successful and beneficial. Without passion, the banker shall do no more than keep the business ticking over, managing it with reasonable efficiency but no more than that. In the same way, an educator can manage a school with reasonable efficiency, but fail to pull moral weight because he or she has no real passion for education. Morality emerges *in the course* of the work as a merchant banker, even in the course of trying to increase profits by backing the right ventures. To see morality as something extrinsic to the job suggests a scenario in which we could have a computer program that checked the morality of what we wrote, as there are programs for checking grammar and spelling and *political correctness*—as if the substance of the work were not itself a matter of morality but needed only occasional monitoring.

This point is important because any serious program of moral education for managers requires us to be clear (as now we are not) about just what moral qualities are intrinsic to good management. A passionate belief that what is being managed has moral importance or value is a prerequisite, because other virtues follow from that: if one has such a belief, one is much more likely to be conscientious, and diligent, creative or imaginative, insightful and well informed. Here, again, a too-narrow concept of *morality* or moral virtue may mislead us; we may, for instance, count diligence as a virtue, but not imagination. But in a wider sense of *morality*, (see Wilson 1987) not all moral virtues – that is, virtues or excellences of character – are under the immediate control of the will (as if morality were only a matter of trying hard and avoiding temptation). We require a list of virtues intrinsic to good management; and to produce such a list we must not have too narrow a concept of *management* (talk of *leadership* or *inspiration* does not help much). We need rather a more general idea of running or controlling some important enterprise – a school, a church, a business, a bank, or anything else. The word *good* in "a good businessperson" should carry as much moral weight as it carries in "a good priest" or "a good teacher" or "a good parent."

Returning to a point made earlier, we can see that the idea of moral education for managers should not be confined to what might be called *in-service training* for existing managers. In schools and higher education, we initiate students into various activities and forms of life, in the hope that they will feel passionate about pursuing some of them. We teach them to engage in games and sports, music, and the arts, and various curricular subjects; and we may even educate them for certain roles, for instance, to be good parents. Many students will in fact become business managers or other kinds of managers and there is every reason to prepare them for that role. Education for potential managers may be as important as education for those who are already managers. We have barely begun to explore this area, which is obviously connected in important ways with the practical training of managers.

Finally, a word about methodology or procedure: We see, first of all, a much less impoverished conception both of *morality* and of *management*, one in which the idea of passion has an important place. But that is only a beginning. We then need a clearer idea of the moral qualities relevant to good management, and a clear idea how much these qualities vary or stay the same relative to that which is being managed (a school, a small business, a giant corporation, or whatever). This task of taxonomy or categorization is to be undertaken by those with experience and insight in various kinds of management, perhaps with the help of analytic philosophers, whose job it is to ensure that the qualities are accurately described in language, so that we know exactly what we are talking about. Thereafter we look to psychologists and other empirical researchers, in conjunction with the practitioners on the ground, to tell us something of how the relevant qualities can be differentiated and fostered; and that will lead to a coherent program of moral education for managers. We will hazard no guesses about what psychological factors may be crucially important; we shall say only that no research is likely to be effective unless it is geared to the centrally important concepts, in particular the concept of *passion*. If we know how to inject passion into management, it might be that we shall have won more than half the battle.

REFERENCES

Hare, R. M. (1981). *Moral thinking*. Oxford: University Press.
Kohlberg, L. (1963). The development of children's orientation toward a moral order. In *Vita Humana*, 6, 9.
Williams, B. A. O. (1985). *Ethics and the limits of philosophy*. London: Fontana.
Wilson, J. (1987). *A preface to morality*. London: Macmillan.
_____. (1990). *A new introduction to moral education*. London: Cassel.
_____. (1995). *Love between equals*. London: Macmillan.

Chapter Four
A Business Perspective on Ethics and Morals

The global and temporal issues of moral management provide a constantly moving target. Accepted practice a century ago isn't tolerated today, at least in the developed world. Even so, one has only to read some of the powerful 19th century literature to realize there was a strong moral compass that wasn't always popular with those in power. Dickens' "A Christmas Carol" can be read as an indictment of crass, miserly anti-humanist management. "Uncle Tom's Cabin," by Harriet Beecher Stowe, helped point out the evils of slavery and introduced the character Simon Legree, a classic example of the bad manager. So, while times and attitudes change, there may yet remain a central core of accepted conduct.

What is a moral manager? Not so many years ago, managing people was a much simpler practice than it is today. It was really more about the "carrot and the stick" or the barter mentality: "you do what I want and you'll receive a reward; otherwise, you'll be punished." This approach worked as long as the employment marketplace was one of a more than sufficient supply of workers to meet the demand. It worked particularly well in the manufacturing environments so prevalent in commerce for centuries. When we consider this approach to management, morality does not appear to play a major role – it's essentially a directive to the employee to "do your job or else." Thus, morality may well have been seen as peripheral to the job of managing rather than intrinsic to it. As long as employees were punctual, not stealing, and putting in a "good day's work," they would receive a paycheck. Is morality then displayed by simply showing up, putting in the effort, and avoiding temptation? As service industries began to flourish and the supply of workers diminished, different professional standards for managers emerged. A trend developed toward a *profession* of management, and this, along with technological advances, meant being more in the public eye. This brought attention to the actions of management and the implications of those actions to shareholders, customers, employees, and even competitors. So rather than business ethics being an ideal to shoot for, it has become a necessity for organizations and its managers.

Since there is basic agreement that business ethics is an imperative, let us review some of what is written about the requirements for ethical/moral leaders and managers.

James Owens writes in his article, "Business Ethics: Age-Old Ideal, Now Real," in 1978:

> Managers of the future, if they are to become or remain such, will be professional in the best sense of the term, including ethical. By a kind of natural evolution, one mark of the future manager will become his unerring

ability to comprehend and evaluate the ethical dimensions of his decisions; lacking this ability and sensitivity to ethical issues, he will be a net liability – and often a latent menace – to his organization." And further, "Few words suffer semantic butchery as does the word 'ethical.' Some regard themselves as ethical if their legal staff can keep them safely within the law. Others feel ethical if they have a generally good 'feeling' toward others – at least on the Sabbath. Still others construe themselves as ethical, even within the turmoil of hard, ambiguous 'business' situations, if they execute exactly the boss's (or a client's) orders (although they might concede that the boss is unethical in some of those orders).

Instead of a constituency, ethics represent a continuity, shared across a wide spectrum of social, economic, managerial and religious positions. It is not that everyone everywhere shares the same definition of right or wrong. It is that everyone everywhere discerns the distinction. Whether you believe ethics are a contrivance of the 'selfish gene,' an automatic response to an intricate social conditioning or the construct humans have inherited from a divine creator, the orientation to do the right thing is a powerful and defining dimension of human nature (Dalla Costa 1998, p. 4).

Ethics may thus represent the character and choices of the individual, but they are expressed and given dimension only in public behavior. Although ethics *flow* from deep personal beliefs, the value of an ethical commitment is realized only in its effect on others and society.

This has always been true, but because of the global economy and global sensibility, the gulf between self and society has never been greater. Ours is the paradox of 'universal intimacy' in which the ethical construct is no longer limited to 'I' and 'thou,' or 'us' and 'them,' but now must embrace the most comprehensive of 'we' (p. 6);

these are the words of John Dalla Costa in his book, *The Ethical Imperative: Why Moral Leadership Is Good Business*.

Princeton sociologist Robert Wuthnow found that for many people with religious faith, ethics in the workplace is reduced to a simple matter of honesty. He argues that this is a very limited view and can lead to an overly simplistic and problematic perspective of "as long as one tells the truth, ethics is not a problem" (Rae and Wong 1996, p. 18).

"…[W]e believe that ethics begins with a rightly ordered soul and with character traits that empower self-restraint and the ability to do things we ought to do…We must also use our reason to help set our moral compasses and to give direction to our character…" state Scott B. Rae and Kenman L. Wong in their book *Beyond Integrity: A Judeo-Christian Approach to Business Ethics* (p. 19).

According to Laura L. Nash in *Good Intentions Aside: A Manager's Guide to Resolving Ethical Problems*, "Business ethics is the study of how personal moral norms apply to the activities and goals of commercial enterprise. It is not a separate moral standard, but the study of how the business context poses its own unique problems for the moral person who acts as an agent of this system" (p. 5).

A Business Perspective on Ethics and Morals

Robert C. Solomon, in *A Better Way to Think about Business: How Personal Integrity Leads to Corporate Success*, tells us,

> Here is ethics 'from the top,' 'handed down' or imposed by a recognized authority (with the power to punish). And so it is natural for us to think of ethics in terms of prohibitions and constraints. But when we think of ethics in this way, whether our response is obedience or rebellion, our ethics is not, in an all-important sense, our own (p. xv).

Jeffrey Seglin, in *The Good, The Bad, and Your Business: Choosing Right When Ethical Dilemmas Pull You Apart*, writes,

> When sophisticated businesspeople try to talk deliberately about ethics, words often become an issue. Though fluent in cost-benefit analyses and accrual accounting methods, when it comes time to articulate thoughts on what constitutes ethical behavior, they use words like *honor, true,* and *duty.* The lack of language to talk about ethical behavior in business stems in part from the fact that the last time these businesspeople discussed issues like this was when they were in the Boy Scouts. Words directly from the Boy Scout code of honor? It's another sign that when it comes to talking about ethics in the workplace, our vocabulary is limited to touchstones from our youth, ones that may no longer feel comfortable. We need a fresh way to talk about the dilemmas we face (p. 8).

But ethics isn't a set of absolute principles, divorced from and imposed on everyday life. Ethics is a way of life, a seemingly delicate but in fact very strong tissue of endless adjustments and compromises. It is the awareness that one is an intrinsic part of a social order, in which the interests of others and one's own interests are inevitably intertwined. And what is business, you should ask, if not precisely that awareness of what other people want and need, and how you yourself can prosper by providing it? Businesses great and small prosper because they respond to people, and fail when they do not respond. To talk about being 'totally ethical' and about 'uneasy compromises' is to misunderstand ethics. Ethics is the art of mutually agreed tentative compromise. Insisting on absolute principles is, if I may be ironic, unethical (p. 11).

Rushworth M. Kidder suggests that finally all ethical decision making is about choices. "Don't' lie, don't cheat, don't steal" says Patrick Gnazzo, vice president of Business Practices at United Technologies Corp. "We all were raised with essentially the same values. Ethics means making decisions that represent what you stand for and not just what the laws are. There is nothing significantly different about cultures around the world that make them more or less honest than others. No culture says to lie, cheat, and steal" (p. 42).

When we look at the roots and definitions of the words *ethic* and *moral* as provided in *Webster's Ninth New Collegiate Dictionary* (1986), we find:

> ethic \ *n* [ME *ethik*, fr. MF *ethique*, fr. L *ethice*, fr. Gk *ethike*, fr. *ethikos*] (14c) 1: *pl but sing or pl in constr*: the discipline dealing with what is good and bad and with

A Business Perspective on Ethics and Morals

moral duty and obligation   2 a: a set of moral principles or values   b: a theory or system of moral values <the present-day materialistic~>   c: pl but sing or pl in constr: the principles of conduct governing an individual or a group   <professional~s>

moral \ *adj* [ME, fr. MF, fr. L *moralis*, fr. *mor-*, *mos* custom – more at MOOD] (14c)   1 a: **of** or relating to principles of right and wrong in behavior : ETHICAL <~judgments>   b: expressing or teaching a conception of right behavior <a~poem>   c: conforming to a standard of right behavior   d: sanctioned by or operative on one's conscience or ethical judgment <a~obligation>   e: capable of right and wrong action <a~agent>   2: probable though not proved L VIRTUAL <a~certainty>   3: having the effects of such on the mind, confidence, or will <a~victory> <~support>

No matter how we define ethic(s) or moral(s), the fact is that corporations are no longer able to close their eyes to their existence and the important role they play in the lives of those associated with the organization. We can no longer excuse our behavior by citing market pressures and the competition. "Corporations are not faceless forces or monoliths. We have to remind and convince ourselves that they are nothing but people and relationships, flesh and blood, working together in cooperation and mutual self-interest, trying – most of them – to do the right thing" (Solomon 1999, p. xx). Yes, corporations have a responsibility to enhance shareholder value, but this cannot be exacted at *any* cost.

THE MORAL MANAGER

Johnson & Johnson is cited over and over again in case studies to demonstrate how companies should behave if they are to be deemed morally responsible. They are world renowned for their actions and are held up as a paragon of morality for the way in which the Tylenol product tampering was handled. They acted responsibly by informing the public and having Tylenol removed from the shelves, after having been informed of a couple of person's deaths. Did the management of J&J have any other choice? The threat of getting caught can be a powerful deterrent, and the threat of disclosure can be a powerful motivator to do the right thing. It is not our intent to minimize the importance of Johnson & Johnson's actions in this situation, but to raise the question of how much of their response is based on altruism. They should, in any case, be lauded for the rapidity of their response to this critical situation, unlike the management at Firestone, which allowed people to continue to drive on their tires with the knowledge that there was a safety issue. What is exemplary about J&J's behavior is that

> By the company's own account, it was not automatically clear to anyone what would be the right thing to do. Even though in the end they were morally and economically sure of their decision, no one could guarantee that the company would recoup its losses in this heavily competitive industry. Nor could it be argued that *not* recalling the product would necessarily incur a costly drop in public confidence in the company. The only way the managers could come to the conclusion *quickly* that a recall was right, given the extreme uncertainty of the situation, was if they had a point of view that respected public safety, valued product reliability, and recognized

A Business Perspective on Ethics and Morals

that good management must be measured in long-term calculations (Nash 1990, p. 42).

Jack Welch, CEO of General Electric, is considered to be one of the top managers in business today. Many others look up to GE for its growth strategies and high shareholder value. Yet GE's list of wrongdoings includes a guilty plea in 1985 to fraud charges for overcharging the Air Force on its Minuteman missile contract; settlement of four civil suits brought by whistleblowers, who alleged that GE cheated the government out of millions of dollars by issuing faulty time cards; a conviction for defrauding the Defense Department by overcharging the Army for a battlefield computer system; a guilty plea to defrauding the Pentagon of more than $30 million in the sale of military jet engines to Israel after an employee received bribes; a patent violation (which GE plans to appeal); and settlement of a lawsuit alleging that they failed to satisfy electrical bonding requirements for its jet engine contracts, thereby creating a safety risk. Corporations exist to increase shareholder value, and GE has certainly fulfilled that obligation (although the return on investment might be considerably higher without all the legal fees involved in the above). But what are we to make of these actions? Is this free enterprise at its finest? What does it say about ethical/moral leadership and management at GE during the twelve years 1985-1997? Is this the type of behavior we should be looking up to and imitating?

What kind of ethics do the oil companies practice? The oil spill of the Exxon Valdez in Prince William Sound off the coast of Alaska left damage that will probably never really be fully repaired even though Exxon committed to spending millions of dollars for cleanup. Besides the devastating environmental damage, each time there's a spill, we as consumers can look forward to increases in our home heating and transportation costs due to a "shortage" of oil!

One of the concerns we as consumers should have is the length of time it takes for the government and most corporations to act morally responsible once information is brought to their attention. Safety advocates allege that the GMC truck has one of the worst safety records of cars and trucks on the road. The Federal Department of Transportation had been conducting a lengthy investigation of GM pickups from the model years 1973 to 1987. They did not require GM to recall the trucks, which they normally do when there are clear safety hazards, but in 1993, they did request that the company voluntarily recall the vehicles because of an alleged flaw in design. The gas tank is located outside the main frame of the truck, presumably making it more prone to explosion. GM refused the recall, which would have included over 4 million pickup trucks, and instead offered $1,000 coupons toward the purchase of a new truck (deemed by some to be a marketing ploy). When is the management of GMC morally and ethically accountable to act on this kind of data — after an ongoing investigation of 14 years?

After all, contends Milton Friedman, *New York Times Magazine*, (13 September 1970, 33, pp. 122-26)

> Business is not a charity...managers of publicly held corporations have a singular responsibility to maximize shareholder wealth. Remember when Ford thought it

A Business Perspective on Ethics and Morals

would be cheaper for them to settle lawsuits rather than recall the ill-fated Pinto? Remember when in the early 1990s many companies were firing faithful employees for the sake of a temporary spike in the price of their stock? (Solomon 1999, p. 22).

We are compelled to ask, "Where do we draw the line?" Of course, there's a "flip side" to consider as well: Should a businessperson refrain from increasing the price of the product in order to contribute to the social objective of preventing inflation, even though a price increase would be in the best interests of the corporation? Should he make expenditures on reducing pollution beyond the amount that is in the best interests of the corporation or that is required by law in order to contribute to the social objective of improving the environment? Should he hire the "hard-core" unemployed instead of better-qualified, available candidates in order to contribute to the social objective of reducing poverty?

If we look at some of the "heroes" of management in best-selling business books today, we may find some of the answers to these questions more readily. How about such noteworthy characters as Attila the Hun and Machiavelli?

> They [these books] are full of enthusiasm for 'Sun-Tze' (the art of war), but they neglect his compatriot Confucius, who knows the real 'secret' of Asian prosperity: *virtue*, integrity, and a real sense of community. This is a phenomenon worth scrutinizing, if only because it highlights a pathology that has come to infect so much of business thinking. The appeal of the books, one surmises, is the overt use of unabashed warrior language.

The Moral Manager

Attila as business hero? Attila was know in his time as 'The Scourge of God.' He was known for his cruelty, for causing widespread death and destruction. To hold up the 'scourge of God' as a leadership hero, to cast him as a role model in business, is surely to set ourselves up for a world that we could only loathe....Consider Niccolo Machiavelli, who, unlike Attila, did not kill anyone. He was, in effect, a brilliant consultant, but like most consultants, he was careful to tell his client, the Prince, what he wanted to hear and what he could use with more or less immediate results. In historical perspective, however, we should be appalled at the changes that Machiavelli (and other Renaissance philosophers) loosed upon the world. What they replaced, in particular, was Aristotle's conception of the honorable statesman, the melding of ethics and politics, the coupling of virtue and living well. Instead, they fanned the flames of self-interest, pure selfishness, a 'war of all against all' (in the words of Thomas Hobbes, one of Machiavelli's best-known English colleagues). Again, it is not the historical details that should interest us here but the question of self-image and identity. Do we want to put our trust in someone who proclaims that his leadership is based on Machiavelli's principles? Why do we honor, even celebrate, such behavior? (Solomon 1999, pp. 5-9).

This choice of "heroes" is particularly distressing in light of the following from the introduction by then House Majority Leader Dick Armey of *Profiles in Character: The Values That Made America:*

> Attention to good character, to standards of right and wrong, even to the study of heroes, seems to be making

A Business Perspective on Ethics and Morals

a comeback. This is encouraging because heroes elevate not only the individual by dint of inspiration, but the larger society as well by reinforcing ideas and virtues necessary for its continuance. If this is true, those in the business world should be greatly concerned about the lack of heroes and those that are being put forward as heroes. Armey goes on to write, Children need to know what deserves to be emulated and loved and nurtured, but knowledge of these things is not transmitted by genes, it must be taught. And perhaps the best way to teach it is to offer real-life examples of men and women who have demonstrated the kind of character we think they should possess.

So, shall we put forward Aaron Feuerstein as business hero, someone for our children to emulate, and whose character we think they should possess? Who is Aaron Feuerstein? Here's his story from *Beyond Integrity: A Judeo-Christian Approach to Business Ethics:*

> ...A recent event that made national headlines involved the moral heroism of Aaron Feuerstein, the owner of a textile mill in New England that manufactures Polartec, a lightweight fabric used to provide warmth in winter clothing. Two weeks before Christmas 1995, the people of the town of Methuen, Massachusetts, watched Malden Mills – one of the last remaining large-scale textile mills in the region and the town's employment and economic lifeline – burn to the ground on a windy night. The fire injured 24 people, left 1,400 workers unemployed, and confirmed fears that the town would be destroyed economically – the plight suffered by many New England towns as other mills were shut down and

relocated in search of lower wage scales. Taking everyone by surprise, the seventy-year-old Feuerstein, who could have simply retired on the insurance money, immediately announced plans to rebuild, with the goal of having his workers back in the mill within a few months. Furthermore, Feuerstein gave every employee a Christmas bonus of $275 and a coupon for food worth $20 at a local supermarket. Amid cheers from his employees, he then announced that for at least the next thirty days he would pay every worker's salary in full and continue their health insurance for the next 90 days. Citing his faith and his belief that difficult circumstances provide the real test of moral convictions, Feuerstein stated that collecting the insurance money and retiring was never a thought that crossed his mind. 'My commitment is to Massachusetts and New England. It's where I live, where I play, where I worship. Malden Mills will rebuild right here,' he said (p. 16).

Aaron Feuerstein or Attila the Hun – whose behavior should we honor and celebrate?

Here's another "heroic" story from the same book:

A well-publicized decision by a leading pharmaceutical company, Merck & Co., offers an equally outstanding example of a publicly held (shareholder-owned) corporation going against the common image of corporations as 'profit at all costs' entities. A number of years ago, a Merck scientist discovered that an adaptation of one of the company's drugs could be used to kill the parasite that causes a disease called river blindness. The disease starts with a seemingly innocuous insect bite that allows the parasites to lay the larvae of worms – which eventually grow to two feet in length – in the body. Over time, these worms produce thousands of microscopic worms. Victims can experience suffering so severe that some elect suicide rather than endure the pain. A common result of the disease is a scarring of the eye that produces blindness. While the discovery of the cure was a cause for celebration, Merck soon found itself in a dilemma: none of the "customers" who needed the drug could afford to pay for it. The disease afflicts mainly people in the Third World, particularly parts of Africa and Central and South America. Merck tried in vain to obtain financial support to help offset the costs of developing the drug and getting it where it was needed. In the end, Merck stayed true to a key element of its company philosophy: "We try never to forget that medicine is for the people. It is not for the profits. The profits follow, and if we remember that, they have never failed to appear. The better we have remembered it, the larger they have been." Merck promised to give the drug away and pay to transport it (at a cost of $20 million per year) to any country that requested it, forever (pp. 16-17).

This behavior is inspiring; this is the kind of behavior we should use to guide our decisions; this is the kind of company in which we can take pride and want to go home and tell our families about in the evening (Scott and Wong 1996).

Marianne Jennings tells us that there are two ways to spot an ethical dilemma: by language and by category.

Here are some key phrases that indicate an ethical dilemma is present and rationalization is underway:

- "Everybody else does it."
- "If we don't do it, someone else will."
- "That's the way it has always been done."
- "We'll wait until the lawyers tell us it's wrong."
- "It doesn't really hurt anyone."
- "The system is unfair."
- "I was just following orders."

No explanation of these is necessary – if we just think about when we might have used one or more of these phrases, we'll recognize a struggle over an appropriate course of action. Jennings refers to this as "the language of ethical lapses" (Jennings 2000).

The second method for spotting an ethical dilemma is to understand the categories of ethical dilemmas. The following twelve categories were developed and listed in *Exchange*, the magazine of Brigham Young University School of Business:

- *Taking things that don't belong to you.* Everything from the unauthorized use of the Pitney-Bowes postage meter at your office for mailing personal letters to exaggerations on travel expenses. Regardless of size, motivation, or the presence of any of the above rationalizations, the unauthorized use of someone else's property or taking property under false pretenses still means taking something that does not belong to you.
- *Saying things you know are not true.* Often in their quest for promotion and advancement, fellow employees discredit their co-workers. Falsely assigning blame or inaccurately reporting conversations is lying. While

"This is the way the game is played around here" is a common justification, saying things that are untrue is an ethical violation.

- *Giving or allowing false impressions.* The salesman who permits a potential customer to believe that his cardboard boxes will hold the customer's tomatoes for long-distance shipping when he knows the boxes are not strong enough has given a false impression. A car dealer who fails to disclose that a car has been in an accident is misleading potential customers. A co-worker or supervisor who takes credit for another employee's idea has allowed a false impression.
- *Buying influence or engaging in conflict of interest.* A company awards a construction contract to a firm owned by the father of the state attorney general while the state attorney general's office is investigating that company. A county administrator responsible for awarding the construction contract for a baseball stadium accepts from contractors interested in bidding on the project paid travel around the country to other stadiums that the contractors have built. The wife of a state attorney general accepts trading advice from the corporate attorney for a highly regulated company and subsequently earns, in her first attempt at the market, over $100,000 in the commodities market in cattle futures. All of these examples illustrate conflicts of interest. Those involved in situations such as these often protest, "But I would never allow that to influence me." The ethical violation is the conflict.

Whether the conflict can or will influence those it touches is not the issue, for neither party can prove conclusively that a *quid pro quo* was not intended. The possibility exists, and it creates suspicion.

- *Hiding or divulging information.* Taking your firm's product development or trade secrets to a new place of employment constitutes an ethical violation: divulging proprietary information. Failing to disclose the results of medical studies that indicate your firm's new drug has significant side effects is the ethical violation of hiding information that the product could be harmful to purchasers.
- *Taking unfair advantage.* Many current consumer protection laws were passed because so many businesses took unfair advantage of those who were not educated or were unable to discern the nuances of complex contracts. Credit disclosure requirements, truth-in-lending provisions, and new regulations on auto leasing all resulted because businesses misled consumers who could not easily follow the jargon of long and complex agreements.
- *Committing acts of personal decadence.* While many argue about the ethical notion of an employee's right to privacy, it has become increasingly clear that personal conduct outside the job can influence performance and company reputation. Thus, a company driver must abstain from substance abuse because of safety issues. Even the traditional company Christmas party and picnic have come under scrutiny as the behavior of

A Business Perspective on Ethics and Morals

employees at, and following, these events has brought harm to others in the form of alcohol-related accidents.
- *Perpetrating interpersonal abuse.* A manager sexually harasses an employee. Another manager is verbally abusive to an employee. Still another manager subjects employees to humiliating correction in the presence of customers. In some cases, laws protect employees. However, many situations are simply ethical violations that constitute interpersonal abuse.
- *Permitting organizational abuse.* Many U.S. firms with operations overseas, such as Levi-Strauss, The Gap, and Esprit, have faced issues of organizational abuse. The unfair treatment of workers in international operations appears in the form of child labor, demeaning wages, and excessively long hours. While a business cannot change the culture of another country, it can perpetuate – or alleviate – abuse through its operations there.
- *Violating rules.* Many rules, particularly those in large organizations that tend toward bureaucracy from a need to maintain internal controls or follow lines of authority, seem burdensome to employees trying to serve customers and other employees. Stanford University experienced difficulties in this area of ethics as it used funds from federal grants for miscellaneous university purposes. Questions arose about the propriety of the expenditures, which quite possibly could have been approved through proper channels, but

weren't. The rules for the administration of federal grant monies used for overhead were not followed. The result was not only an ethical violation but damage to Stanford's reputation and a new president for the university.

- *Condoning unethical actions.* In this breach of ethics, the wrong results from the failure to report the wrong. What if you witnessed a fellow employee embezzling company funds by forging her signature on a check that was to be voided? Would you report that violation? A winking tolerance of others' unethical behavior is in itself unethical. Suppose that as a product designer you were aware of a fundamental flaw in your company's new product; a product predicted to catapult your firm to record earnings. Would you pursue the problem to the point of halting the distribution of the product? Would you disclose what you know to the public if you could not get your company to act?
- *Balancing ethical dilemmas.* In these types of situations, there are no right or wrong answers; rather, there are dilemmas to be resolved. For example, Levi-Strauss struggled with its decision about whether to do business in the People's Republic of China because of known human rights violations by the government there. Other companies debated doing business in South Africa when that country's government followed a policy of apartheid. In some respects, the presence of these companies would help by advancing human rights and, certainly, by improving the standard of living for at least some international operations workers.

On the other hand, their ability to recruit businesses could help such governments sustain themselves by enabling them to point to economic successes despite human rights violations (Jennings 2000, pp. 48-54).

How do businesses hire personnel ethically, and train managers in ethics and morals? Do they? Should they? Let us look at an interview situation where the hiring manager is interested in ascertaining the morality of the interviewee and thus asks a question such as, "Would you please give me a few examples of your moral character?" Or "How do I know that you're moral and will, in fact, act ethically in this particular job in this particular environment?" We could imagine the Equal Employment Opportunity Commission and the American Civil Liberties Union might have some concerns about these questions. Are they relevant to the workplace? One wonders how William Jefferson Clinton might have responded to these questions! Clinton exhibits an extremely strong work ethic, but we would be stretching the truth to speak of his moral leadership. Nonetheless, he did carry out the duties of the job.

So, what should we look for in a prospective employee – the ability to act ethically or the ability to be moral? If an individual reaches the age of entering the workforce and has no morals, will we ever be able to train him into morality? We think not, particularly in light of the fact that so many people today think the term *business ethics* is an oxymoron. The definition of moral includes "expressing or teaching a conception of right behavior" and "conforming to a standard of right behavior." What is *right behavior* in the workplace? Who decides? Who judges?

The Moral Manager

According to Anna-Maija Lamsa on Web Forum's Business and Leadership Ethics, Subject: Postmodernism in business ethics,

> Virtue ethics say that those who decide are those who establish codes or standards of professional conduct for the relevant actor. These codes may be based on principle, purpose, or consequence (or any combination), but they also take into account the characteristics of the situation. One's peers are the deciders of 'truth,' at least for each other. This appears to be a middle ground between the universal principles and situational ethics that says there are no universal principles. The peers achieve a consensus around a principle or norm of behavior, although different groups may adopt different norms.
>
> Many new managers today are strongly committed to the idea of self-expression and independence. It is crucial for top leadership in today's corporation to take a more active role in setting high, meaningful, other-oriented moral standards for the rest of its employee group and to show how good business questions and personal conscience go hand in hand. This cannot be done with platitudes. Nor can it be done with utopian generalizations about business ethics. It must be achieved by a frank reexamination of those common, everyday problems that put the business person's basic values on the line, often without he or she noticing. (Nash 1990, p. 248)

If we as individuals are faced with an ethical dilemma and it comes down to our job versus our individual principles or ethics, which will fall? Do we stick to our individual principles because we fear getting caught? How much peer pressure is being brought to bear?

> If we've learned nothing else in the 1980s, it is that business ethics will not go away. It is here already, at the heart of every economic transaction, resource allocation, and human resource decision. The issues are difficult and the track record filled with failures even by the well intentioned. Future threats to traditional ways of doing business from sudden ownership disruptions to new alliances with foreigners whose values and culture may differ from ours – only sharpen the need for a coherent and practical approach to achieving high standards of business conduct (Nash 1990, p. xiv).

Nash also writes that

> Up to now, management concern about ethics has seemed to center on two great fears: the fear that living up to ethical obligations will impose an immediate cost on the bottom line, and the fear that employees who adopt unethical standards will pose a financial liability down the road (p. xii).

There are many approaches and methodologies to training employees in business ethics. For some, it's a simple statement of "Just do the right thing." Unfortunately, many of the ethical dilemmas we face today in business are not a question of right versus wrong, but of right versus right, where one "right" value is pitted against another "right" value.

The Moral Manager

Kidder asks us to consider that:
- It is right to find out all you can about your competitor's costs and price structures – and right to obtain information only through proper channels.
- It is right to resist the importation of products made in developing nations to the detriment of the environment – and right to provide jobs, even at low wages, for citizens of those nations.
- It is right to "throw the book" at good employees who make dumb decisions that endanger the firm – and right to have enough compassion to mitigate the punishment and give them another chance.

The *really* tough choices don't center on right versus wrong. "They are genuine dilemmas precisely because each side is firmly rooted in one of our basic, core values." And further,

> When good people encounter tough choices, it is rarely because they're facing a moral temptation. Only those living in a moral vacuum will be able to say, 'On the one hand is the good, the right, the true, and noble. On the other hand is the awful, the wicked, the false, and the base. And here I stand, equally attracted to each.' If you've already defined one side as a flat-out, unmitigated 'wrong,' you don't usually consider it seriously. Faced with the alternatives of arguing it out with your boss or gunning him down in the parking lot, you don't see the latter as an option. For most people, some sober reflection is all that's required to recognize a wolf-like moral temptation masquerading in the lamb's clothing of a seeming ethical dilemma (Kidder 1996, p. 18).

A Business Perspective on Ethics and Morals

If we return to Wuthnow's finding that for many people with religious faith, ethics in the workplace is reduced to a simple matter of honesty, he himself argues that with such a limited view, "one's behavior may contribute to the burning of rain forests and the perpetuation of world hunger and yet, as long as one tells the truth, ethics is not a problem" (Rae and Wong 1996, p. 18).

Some of the more *simplistic* approaches may not be enough in training our employees in business ethics and morality today; it isn't enough to tell managers to consult their moral intuitions and instincts and then take the course of action that they can live with in good conscience.

According to a recent survey, the U.S. public is worried that tomorrow's leaders are missing some crucial lessons today. A snapshot of people's concerns, taken from a recent poll in Illinois by the Gallup Organization for the Institute for Global Ethics, conducted in mid-1999 (see Appendix A), shows that *over 70% disagree or strongly disagree* with the statement, "You can be an effective leader without being ethical," while 15% agree or strongly agree with the statement. Approximately *75% agree or strongly agree* with the statement, "People today are not learning the values they should."

> The problems of business today are, first and foremost, profoundly ethical and philosophical problems. They are questions about the very nature of the business enterprise and the nature of the corporation. For example, the very conception of the corporation as a 'legal fiction' defined in terms of its obligations to its stockholders implies that corporations are not moral or

morally responsible agencies and suggests (at best) a morally ambiguous sense of responsibility for the executives and employees of the corporation (Solomon 1999, p. xxi).

Thinking in terms of 'making money' and 'the market,' devoid of any larger sense of obligation or ethics, never made any country or culture 'great.' Indeed, such crudely self-interested thinking is what marks countries and cultures for destruction. But the argument doesn't really change when it gets shifted to the infamous 'obligation to the stockholders.' Not a week goes by without some socially destructive corporate act or policy being defended in those terms, as if that single obligation closed the question. But what gives us hope is that the executives of those corporations are for the most part not at all happy with such decisions, even when they feel obliged to make them. They know full well that their obligation to the stockholders is not exclusive, that it does not eclipse their other obligations, that it does not substitute for their sense of their own integrity or compensate for its loss. But a combination of established dogma, shortsighted legal liabilities, legislative cowardice and corruption, and lack of public awareness, education, and imagination contrive to maintain this singular and ultimately destructive sense of obligation in even the very best CEOs and corporate directors (Solomon, p. 123).

Businesses cannot sit back and hope that when new employees join the organization that their behavior will be

A Business Perspective on Ethics and Morals

ethical and moral, believing that these things are learned at home, at school, etc.

> Ethical behavior must be based on a strong moral foundation, including personal moral development and an organizational structure that encourages and rewards desired ethical action. The pressures of competition must be understood and coped with to improve ethical behavior. The idea that ethics is learned at home, in school and in church does not recognize the impact of the organization on ethical decision makers. Today there is an increasing need for professional associations and corporations to promote and to enforce codes of ethics and eliminate unethical conduct (Rae and Wong 1996, p. 601).

It is critically important that companies establish a code of ethical conduct, a written policy that provides basic guidelines and informs all employees around the globe that there is a commitment on the company's part to ethical behavior. But a written policy or code of ethical conduct is *not* enough. We must make the investment in training our managers and leaders, as well as others, and this should not be a "one-shot deal;" the training should be ongoing, reinforcing the commitment to ethical behavior on at least an annual basis. As stated in an earlier chapter of this book, "So we ... [make the decision] to aim rather at giving our clients certain items of mental *equipment* whereby they are to make up their own minds about moral issues." This precludes the need for basing "our moral education on a particular moral *content*, the need to specifically define what moral is and means." It would be impossible to cover all the specific situations that might arise putting us into ethical or moral dilemmas, so providing the *equipment* or *tools* for us to utilize makes good sense. We need guidelines for making these choices, some process to go through to help us understand how to *apply* general ethical standards.

> It's not that we need to have all right answers. It's that we want to be able to understand and explain (if not to our board, employees, owners, or co-managers, then to ourselves) why we did what we did. We don't want to justify our actions in the sense that we make excuses for them. We want to justify them as thoughtful reactions to difficult dilemmas. That's pretty much what ethical decision-making is all about and, when viewed in this way, regardless of what we call it, it becomes clear that we do some of this every waking hour of every day of our business lives. Some dilemmas are just a tad more difficult than others to navigate (Seglin 2000, p. 21).

When considering what types of programs to develop and implement, a review of the three levels in Lawrence Kohlberg's theory of moral development might prove useful:

Level I – Pre-conventional
- Oriented toward punishment
- Defers to power
- Actions should satisfy needs (self)

Level II – Conventional
- Emphasizes conformity and acceptance to gain approval
- Concern with fixed rules

Level III – Post-conventional
- Moral orientation toward more principled life
- Seeking higher moral ground
- Concerned about the individual and the collective
- Principles are:
  - Logical
  - Comprehensive
  - Universal
  - Consistent
  - Aligned

Most programs today tend to be compliance oriented, making them pre-conventional or conventional. We should be able to agree that in the business world, we'd want people at the post-conventional level. We need training programs that help us get them there (Kohlberg 1963).

In *Ethics in Organizations*, David Murray observes that

> from the start it must be emphasized that there can be no rigid, structured method that will automatically give us 'right' answers. We will at many stages be confronted with the need to make judgments. Not everything is quantifiable. Not everything is predictable. We should, however, be able to structure and record our judgments so that our eventual decisions are at the very least explicable, even if not to everyone justifiable (p. 113).

There are many in the field of business ethics who have developed models for our use, from the simplistic to the extremely complex. Let's look at some of them:

"One stems from Immanuel Kant's categorical imperative, loosely similar to the Golden Rule of 'Do unto others as

The Moral Manager

you would have them do unto you.' Treating others or others' money as we would want to be treated is a powerful evaluation technique in ethical dilemmas," according to Marianne M. Jennings (2000) in *Business: Its Legal, Ethical and Global Environment* (p. 56).

The late Dr. Norman Vincent Peale and management expert Kenneth Blanchard offer three questions that managers should ponder in resolving ethical dilemmas:

1. Is it legal? If the answer to this question is no, the manager should proceed no further.
2. Is it balanced? This allows the manager to step back and gain some perspective on the problem – how does it affect others such as employees, shareholders, the community, etc.?
3. How does it make me feel? This requires a manager to do a self-examination of the comfort level of a decision. Some decisions, though they may be legal and may appear balanced, can still make a manager uncomfortable (p. 55).

A very simple model asks the manager or decision maker to think about whether he/she would take this action if it were going to appear on the front page of a local or national newspaper the next day.

Business ethicist Laura Nash has developed a series of questions that business managers should ask themselves as they evaluate their ethical dilemmas. One of the questions is: "How would I view the issue if I stood on the other side of the fence?" Other questions in the Nash model include: "Am I able to discuss my decision with my family, friends, and those closest to me?" "What am I trying to accomplish with my decision?" "Will I feel as comfortable about my decision over time as I do today?" (pp. 55-56).

The *Wall Street Journal* model for resolution of ethical dilemmas consists of compliance, contribution, and consequences. Like the Blanchard-Peale model, any proposed conduct must first be in compliance with the law. The next step requires an evaluation of a decision's contributions to the shareholders, the employees, the community, and the customers. Finally, managers are asked to envision the consequences of a decision, such as whether headlines that are unfavorable to the firm may result (Jennings 2000, p. 56).

Rushworth Kidder (1996) has listened to and analyzed hundreds of ethical dilemmas and provides us with three principles drawn from the traditions of moral philosophy.

Of the many theories that have been propounded for ethical decision making, these represent three that are particularly useful in helping us think through right-versus-right issues. Each gives us a way to test the twin rights of a dilemma. Each has a long and noble tradition behind it. For clarity, we'll give them three shorthand labels: *ends-based*, *rule-based*, and *care-based*.

Here's the gist of each:

Ends-based thinking. Known to philosophers are utilitarianism, this principle is best known by the maxim *Do whatever produces the greatest good for the greatest number*. It demands of us a kind of cost-benefit analysis, determining who will be hurt and who helped and measuring the intensity of that help. It is the staple of public policy debate; most legislation, these days, is crafted with this utilitarian test in mind. At the heart of this principle is an assessment of consequences, a forecasting of outcomes. Philosophers typically refer to utilitarianism, in fact, as a form of consequentialism – or, more precisely, as a teleological principle, from the Greek word *teleos*, meaning 'end' or 'issue.' Why? Because you cannot determine the "greatest good" without speculating on probable futures. Hence the "ends-based" label, Utilitarianism, examines possible results and picks the one that produces the most benefit over the greatest range.

Rule-based thinking. Often associated with the name of the German philosopher Immanuel Kant, this principle is best known by what Kant somewhat obtusely called "the categorical imperative." Kant put it this way: "Act only on that maxim through which you can at the same time will that it should become a universal law." Simply put, that means, "Follow only the principle that you want everyone else to follow." In other words, act in such a way that your actions could become a universal standard that others ought to obey. Ask yourself, "If *everyone in the world* followed the rule of action I am following, would that create the greatest good or [in Kant's words] the greatest 'worth of character'?" This mode of thinking stands directly opposed to utilitarianism. Arguing that consequentialism is hopelessly flawed – how, after all, can we *ever* imagine we know the entire consequences of our actions? – the rule-based thinker pleads for acting only in accord with fixed rules. Never mind outcomes: stick to your principles and let the consequential chips fall where they may. Based firmly on duty – on what we ought to do, rather than what we think might work – it is known among philosophers as deontological thinking, from the Greek word *deon*, meaning 'obligation' or 'duty.'

Care-based thinking. Putting love for others first, this third principle comes into play most frequently in the Golden Rule: *Do unto others what you like them to do to you.* It partakes of a feature known to philosophers as reversibility: In other words, it asks you to test your actions by putting yourself in another's shoes and imagining how it would feel if you were the recipient, rather than the perpetrator, of your actions. Often associated with Christianity – Jesus, after all, said, "All things whatsoever ye would that men should do to you, do ye even so to them" (Matt. 7:12) – it is in fact so universal that it appears at the center of every one of the world's great religious teachings. While some philosophers (including Kant) have disputed its standing as a practical principle, it is for many people the only rule of ethics they know, deserving consideration for the moral glue it has provided over the centuries.

The usefulness of these principles is not that they will deliver an airtight answer to your dilemma. They are not part of a magic answer kit that produces infallible solutions: If they were, ethics would be infinitely easier than it is, and the moral problems of the world would have been satisfactorily sorted out centuries ago. No, the principles are useful because they give us a way to exercise our moral rationality. They provide different lenses through which to see our dilemmas, different screens to use in assessing them (Kidder 1996, p. 26).

REFERENCES

Dalla Costa, J. (1998). *The ethical imperative: Why moral leadership is good business.* Reading, Massachusetts: Perseus Books.
Jennings, M. M. (2000). *Business: Its legal, ethical and global environment.* Cincinnati, Ohio: West Legal Studies in Business/Thomson Learning.
Kidder, R. M. (1996). *How good people make tough choices: Resolving the dilemmas of ethical living.* New York: Morrow.
Murray, D. (1997). *Ethics in organizations.* London: Kogan.
Nash, L. L. (1990). *Good intentions aside: A manager's guide to resolving ethical problems.* Boston, Massachusetts: Harvard Business School Press.
Osborne, R. (2000). "A matter of ethics at United Technologies Corp.: The rules are clear: 'Don't lie, don't cheat, don't steal.'" *Industry Week* 249 (14) (4 Sep): 41-42.
Owens, J. (1978). "Business ethics: Age-old ideal, now real." *Business Horizons.* (Bloomington: Indiana University) v. 21.
Rae, S. B. & Wong, K. L. (1996). *Beyond integrity: A Judeo-Christian approach to business ethics.* Grand Rapids, Michigan: Zondervan Publishing House.
Sashkin, M. (1984). "Participative management is an ethical imperative." *Organizational Dynamics* 12 (4) (Spring): 4-23.

Seglin, J. L. (2000). *The Good, the bad, and your business: Choosing right when ethical dilemmas pull you apart.* New York: Wiley & Sons, Inc.

Solomon, R. C. (1999). *A better way to think about business: How personal integrity leads to corporate success.* New York: Oxford University Press.

Chapter Five

Universal Moral and Ethical Education, Cultural Approaches, and A Roadmap for the Moral Manager in Applying Business Ethics

The previous chapter indicated in general the difficulties of doing business ethically. In this chapter, an overview is provided of the context and content of universal moral and ethical education, along with multiple maps of cultural approaches to the topic. We then move to the individual and what it means to be a moral manager. The information provided may be considered a checklist, roadmap, or guide to the thoughtful expression of the art of the ethical or moral manager.

1. UNIVERSAL MORAL AND ETHICAL EDUCATION

A baseline of core values and principles is present in all world cultures or world religions. To implement a universal ethic or moral education standard, these values must be defined, understood and embraced. A global ethic or standard requires developing and implementing core values which include (1) the dignity of the person, (2) freedom, (3) communal responsibility, and (4) intergenerational concern for individuals and the environment. People are not self-contained atoms; they work together, cooperate, compete and interact in many ways. Culture connects us with one another and makes the development of the individual possible. It is culture that defines how people relate to nature and their physical environment, and through which we express our attitudes to and beliefs in other forms of life. It is the responsibility of the moral educator to inculcate these priorities in any moral education program. This is particularly challenging when dealing with business, even though the production of goods and services often eclipses concern for the person. Concern for the person, even though institutionalized as human resources, must remain both paramount and ubiquitous.

Analysis of corporate culture or personality refers to a study of how different ways of living together affect the enhancement of human choices and productivity. These dynamics are clearly evident in today's business world. A corporation is not static or changeless; it is in a constant state of flux—influencing and being influenced by internal and external elements of the broader culture. Business reaches into every component of our lives, and the manager today is expected to be proactive in all the outreach arenas. A good manager reflects the company's culture, which in turn reflects the corporation's history, institutions and attitudes, social movements, conflicts, struggles, and political concerns. The corporation is dynamic and evolving, remaining accountable to both the culture in which it resides and to the people working within it.

As a result of accelerated change, the impact of diverse cultures, mass communication, education, and changes in family life, traditional corporate cultures have been disrupted and leveled. Thus, the dominant powers within a culture become unstable and unpredictable. Amidst all of these changes, the manager is still expected to function as leader, motivator, and moral model and in a host of other more technical roles.

Research has established that it is the tension within the corporation, and the creativity to which this tension gives rise, that makes many companies innovative, dynamic and enduring. Appreciation and enhancement of this tension is a cornerstone of any ethical culture and the foundation of moral education; it is also the newly emerging role for the moral manager. The moral manager is called upon not only to appreciate, but also to implement and enhance awareness of, differences and tensions as synergetic sources of energy, rather than necrotic elements. The modern manager is called upon to manage these tensions, not extinguish them.

Managers have crucial ethical responsibilities within their own companies. In the absence of an ideally integrated and agreed upon norm, the attainment of some measure of order and the realization of the basic moral values vitally depends on the existence of commonly held values capable of preserving order and securing those values within their jurisdictions. Corporate governance and management must be the chief architects seeking to erect and maintain a consensual agreement on norms, values and principles that will govern the tactical and strategic concerns of the corporation.

There is a growing demand for forms of democratic participation in all corporations. While the main responsibility of addressing generic problems clearly lies with the board, management and workers often offer diverse points of view. Enhancing worker participation is now seen as a function of the manager and does not challenge the pre-eminence of the board and stockholders. It does, however, give rise to new challenges, which must now be managed. Properly guided, it can energize corporate life and become a resource to the board and stockholders alike.

While free, fair and regular assessment, freedom of information, and freedom of association constitute basic ingredients of life in any moral corporation, these must be supplemented by corporate safeguards protecting individual, political, ethnic and other minorities against undue pressure for rigid and unnecessary conformance. In a world in which 10,000 distinct societies live in roughly 200 states, the question of how to accommodate minorities is not of academic interest only, but is a central challenge to any humane politics. It is also the challenge of any effective manager.

Powerful trends towards globalization have not erased individual desires of workers claiming self-determination within the workplace. Too often management is inclined to react with discrimination and repression to cultural minorities insisting on their identity and demanding some form of self-determination within corporate life. The desire of cultural minorities to assert their cultural identity or give it political expression in some form of autonomy must be taken seriously so long as it is consistent with the overall mission and goals of the corporation. Members belonging to minorities must enjoy the same basic rights and freedoms, and the same safeguards granted to others. In addition, whatever form of management is established, the human rights of all members of majorities and minorities alike must be guaranteed. Furthermore, tolerance and cultural conviviality should be promoted, encouraging cultural diversity so that the various groups can make a significant contribution to the corporate mission. Experience warns that corporate politics are sometimes used as a means to sow discord and conflict rather than forge mutual understanding and respect. When this occurs, not only is the company's mission damaged but moral integrity is impugned.

The principles and values embodied in a universal ethic must be seen as a moral minimum to be observed by all without qualification. Those basic standards, such as individual dignity, do not suffice to resolve all international and global issues that involve ethical or moral questions. A case in point—individual dignity cannot answer what constitutes fair trade or how the costs of eliminating environmentally damaging technologies should be distributed among the countries concerned.

Though problems of justice and fairness are undoubtedly central to a universal moral education, it is not possible to solve them by philosophical fiat because a simple and generally accepted principle of justice does not exist. Justice and fairness in transnational corporations cannot be found by imposing some preconceived moral principle on the company. In this situation, all parties must be allowed to have a say. All affected parties must be represented and have a voice in what principles or rules should decide the matter. There should be a commitment to building a culture of peace and harmony that is not at odds with effective corporate profit making. The culture of peace is not just a theory or a set of principles. Culture of peace, as Frederico Mayor has said, "is a process by which positive attitudes to peace, democracy and tolerance are forged through education and knowledge about different cultures." It is a process that is built on the proactive stance of peace building: preventive action before a conflict has broken out and corrective action after it has taken its human toll. It involves the participation of all parties engaged in any conflict, the fostering of democratic process and respect for rights, and non-violent management of conflicts.

A pluralistic attitude is not only desirable but also realistic if dangerous conflicts are to be avoided. A greater awareness of the complex nature of corporate life and of the need for a more tolerant attitude to value differences must be explored. Cooperation between different peoples with different interests and from different value cultures will be facilitated and conflict kept within acceptable and even constructive limits, if participants can see themselves as being bound and motivated by shared commitments. It is imperative to look for a core of shared ethical values and principles.

Universal Moral and Ethical Education

Universal moral education promulgates that all human beings are born equal and that they enjoy these rights irrespective of class, gender, race, community or generation. This implies that the basic necessities for a decent life must be the foremost concern of companies and governments. A company's long-term future clearly derives from its components of integrity and trustworthiness, which goes beyond simple financial concerns. The morally educated manager must take care of and use the environmental, cultural and natural resources for the benefit of all members of present and future generations.

Each generation is a custodian and a potential enhancer of humanity's common and cultural heritage and must leave for future generations at least the same opportunity that it has enjoyed. International efforts to find ways to stop the depletion of the ozone layer and cope with the greenhouse effect demonstrate a willingness to resort to scientific method in order to solve empirical dispute and to involve various points of view and discussion. This trend may be supportive of a global ethics that emphasizes truthfulness, respect for the facts and objectivity that contrasts with the willfulness that is still far too pervasive in politics. The bonds of global non-governmental organizations, voluntary societies, grassroots organizations, churches and other religious associations, action groups, professional societies, interest groups and similar institutions forge links that bypass national frontiers and loyalties. They constitute the core of any future world citizenship, even though their loyalties may be confined to quite narrow issues or specialized interests. They can mobilize world opinion in order to draw attention to global problems, as some environmental or human rights groups have successfully done.

People have always differed in their political visions. Influenced by their cultural heritage and historical experience, they often have different views about what further values their society should uphold and what specific projects it should pursue. Expressly acknowledging such diversity, a global ethics provides the minimal requirement any government and people must meet, but otherwise leaves scope for political creativity, social imagination and cultural pluralism.

Confining a global ethics to certain basic principles and criteria also reflects awareness that societies do not, need not, and cannot follow identical developmental patterns and styles. While insisting on a number of fundamental normative standards, a global ethics abstains from committing societies to one, and only one, path on which to advance. This must be understood in managing corporations that arise from distinctly different cultures.

Securing a better future for all may involve sacrifices and require profound changes in attitudes and behavior; these will accompany and reflect changes in people's social priorities, the educational system, the patterns of consumption, and even the most basic beliefs about how the individual should relate to society and the earth. Boards of Trustees, managers, governments, and political leaders will have to play a crucial role in convincing their citizens of the need for change and in suggesting novel political, economic, and social strategies. Such obligations, though daunting, remain essential.

Cooperation between different peoples with different interests and from different cultures will be facilitated, and conflict kept within acceptable and even constructive limits, if participants can see themselves as being bound and motivated by shared commitments. It is, therefore, imperative to look for a core of shared ethical values and principles. The individual charged with this search process is the moral manager. From these various values, the manager will weave a web of relationships that will bind the members together and move the corporate mission ahead as well.

A global ethics should be developed that applies equally to all those involved in corporate and world affairs. Its efficacy will depend on the ability of people and companies to transcend narrow self-interest and agree that the interests of humanity as a whole will be best served by acceptance of a set of common rights and responsibilities. The values and principles of a global ethics should be the shared points of reference, providing the minimal moral guidance the world must heed in its manifold efforts to tackle the global issues outlined above.

From what we have been discussing, it is clear that the creation of a global ethics remains a formidable task. However, some headway has been made. In all religious and ethical traditions, certain assumptions appear universal. Primary among these is the "Golden Rule" that others are to be treated with the respect that we would ourselves expect. This is universally codified and reflected in Zoroasterism, Confucianism, Jainism, Buddhism, Hinduism, Judaism, Mohammadism and Baha'ism, as well as New Age ethics.

As these visions of humanity are explored, it becomes clear that certain foundational principles follow, which at a minimum include:
1. Humans are free and have inherent dignity.
2. This dignity requires respect.
3. Since we live in communities (nations, etc.), we have responsibility (duties) for one another and ourselves.
4. Human dignity requires respect, which presumes that one, ought not to kill.
5. The dignity and duty of humanity is to insure that all peoples have the basic necessities of life, which requires dealing honestly with each other. (This is not necessarily antithetical to successful entrepreneurship.)
6. Tolerance for diversity is a pre-condition for the possibility of human interaction and global business.

Interconnectedness involves a sharing of resources. Although governments are clearly involved in creating a global ethics, the role of business organizations also must be considered. All of the ethical components discussed here need to be incorporated into the treatment of human resources within organizations and in organizations that interact through business partnerships.

2. CULTURAL APPROACHES TO MORAL EDUCATION AND ETHICS: MULTIPLE MAPS

There are of course a semi-infinite number of approaches to any *applied* moral education and ethics. While universalizability and reversibility remain standard demands

Universal Moral and Ethical Education

of any ethic, when these concerns are dealt with *in situ*, such clarity becomes highly elusive.

Perhaps the clearest application of ethical principles in life and work involves the concept of "integrity" as its measure. Daigneault (1999) argues that:

> Our challenge now is to expand our focus to include all integrity. We have not abandoned ethics or compliance. Just as many organizations over the years have broadened their compliance programs to include a commitment to ethics, we are now urging the next step in this progression. Building upon a solid foundation for integrity.

In an attempt to implement this concept of integrity as an essential of any universal global ethics or moral education, Vogel and Taylor of the ERC Fellows Program global research team, identified eight categories of components of integrity: the "rule of law; free-market systems and structures; corporate ethics and compliance standards; labor issues; environmental issues; national cultural issues; local community issues; and human rights issues" (Vogel and Taylor 1999). These components conform to the Kantian criteria while grounding them in application. There are practical advantages that issue from the use of the concept of integrity and its constituent values: companies perceived as manifesting these core values usually have greater access to financial reward, community support, better employee morale and a better reputation. Such companies are perceived as having "integrity"—a hallmark of the morally educated individual and morally appropriate corporation.

This component of integrity is compelling and more than just window dressing. Federal Reserve Chairman, Alan Greenspan said to the Gerald R. Ford Foundation in Grand Rapids, Michigan, "It is decidedly not true that 'nice guys finish last'". Greenspan adds,

> Trust is at the root of any economic system based on mutually beneficial exchange...In virtually all transactions, we rely on the word of those with whom we do business...If a significant number of business people violated the trust upon which our interactions are based, our court system and our economy would be swamped into immobility. (Greenspan 1999).

Each tradition will approach the definition of integrity and moral/ethical education from within its own context. For all the cultural differences that abound in our world, there appear to be clear and recurring principles, which inform all traditions. We now turn to brief encapsulations to give the reader a flavor for the divergence and convergence of major moral traditions.

The Jewish Experience

In an article, Rabbi Yitzchok Breitowitz (http://www.jlaw.com/Articles/JewBusEthl.html) introduces the concept of Jewish business ethics and its obligation upon the Jewish manager.

> Many of us have a mistaken idea of what is within the compass or scope of our religious traditions. People know that lighting Chanukah candles is something you

talk about with a rabbi, observance of the Shabbat…but many people have an attitude that if I don't tell the rabbi how to run his business, the rabbi shouldn't tell me how to run mine. Very often we live fragmented, dichotomized lives in which what we do in the office from 9 to 5…is our own private affair and then at home we observe the holidays…

The rabbi makes a compelling argument that in the Torah there is a contextual juxtaposition between the religious and ritual demands and ethical obligations between peoples. A separation of ritual from life is neither feasible nor possible. All morality and ethical demands are derived from an encounter with the divine, and as such, separation of law from life is alien. At the highest levels, one is expected to do more than observe the letter of the law. It is demanded that the individual often transcend the letter of the law in favor of the spirit of it. Compelling commentaries and stories are abundant in which the rabbis adjudicate issues in ways surprising to the pure rationalist.

The various texts and web sites are clear that an egocentric approach to individual rights simply does not suffice within the religious tradition, which is based on a community of believers united beyond the bonds of simple convenience. Nor is one expected, within the Jewish tradition, to relinquish possessions. Rather, it is how one conducts business that reflects the individual's commitment to God and the community. Business ethics is a particularly demanding area because it is the place where the worlds collide.

The ethical and moral literature is voluminous and the individual is not left to wander without direction. There is clear instruction to the seeker. The commentators intriguingly stress concern with stealing and defamation of competitors. In moving and enlightening passage after passage, the message is made clear: the Jewish business person is a member of a larger community that demands accountability, integrity, service and honesty as a condition for the possibility of genuine adherence to Torah. The call is to an abundant life in which the person integrates their personal, religious and corporate life into an authentic and integrated whole.

The Christian Experience

The Christian approach to moral education and business ethics is an elaboration of the Judaic tradition. In his book, *Honesty, Morality and Conscience*, published by NavPress, Jerry White summarizes five essential guidelines for conducting business (White 1978).

These guidelines include the Deuteronomic demand (Deut 25: 13-15) to give full amount in exchange for a fair payment. The dominating theme here is integrity and the recognition that one is working not only to provide income and create value, but also to give glory to God in Jesus Christ.

The second demand is honesty, a full and complete disclosure of the reality with our employers, co-workers, employees and customers…in short, to all stakeholders.

This honesty will have implications for our use of time and resources as well as our achievements.

The third requirement is to be a servant. The dominating theme is Matthew 20:28 in which Christ has come to serve, not to be served. The importance and added value of our activities lies in our service. This is a unique perspective in which the needs of others are seen as preceding our own.

The fourth requirement is personal accountability and responsibility. In short, we are asked to be responsible for our lives and our actions. We are "in the world but not of the world". We are to be co-creators with God and not passively shaped by the world's demands.

The last of White's categories includes the notion of reasonable profitability. This is a rather tricky concept and requires significant definitional analysis and examination. Individuals will be asked to assess a reasonable profit in their own way. A suggested approach is one in which the needs and rights of others enjoy the same status as our own. While this flies in the face of much contemporary thinking, it is fundamental to any religious view of economic transaction.

Beyond what can be designated, as in every religious tradition, a Christian approach to moral education involves a mystical element. That is to say, individuals form their lives as a result of their encounter with a caring and living God in the person of Jesus Christ. Each religious approach will have its own version of this, but its presence in every model is unmistakable, even though sometimes highly skewed culturally.

THE MORAL MANAGER

The Islamic Vision

In *Islamic Business Ethics* (1996), Dr. Rafik Beekun summarizes an approach to ethical and moral education by designation of various components of the believer's life and work. Each stakeholder is addressed.

The believer is commanded to behave Islamically toward *customers* by provision of the best quality goods and services. This implies modest cost and compliance with the requirements of integrity. No one is to be denied service or goods based on accidental concerns such as race, religion, etc.

The practicing Islamic businessperson maintains consistency in quality and service, as well as a fair profit in dealing with *suppliers and distributors*. Any inappropriate inducements are to be deplored.

One is to act justly to *employees* as well. Employee safety and working conditions are important, as is the demand for a just wage. Employees can expect to be provided opportunity to develop their skills and safeguard their rights to privacy. Good faith is expected in all interpersonal and business transactions.

Competitors are to be competed with fairly and monopoly is to be avoided.

Stockholders must be guaranteed a fair return on investment. Resources are not to be wasted and employees are to be compensated fairly.

The broader *community* of the Muslim world is to be supported as well as the local community. Good citizenship is expected of an individual, as well as welcoming one's obligation to help the needy. Natural resources are to be honored.

In all things, honesty is paramount. In fact, the disappearance of honesty is seen as a sign of the imminence of the Day of Judgment. As the prophet has said:

> When honesty is lost, then wait for the hour. The person said, "How will that be lost?" The prophet (peace be upon him) said, "When the power or authority comes in the hands of unfit persons, then wait for the Hour." (Beekun 1996)

What we have provided in these three traditions of ethical and moral education is simply a listing of the most compelling arguments. More detailed analysis is beyond the scope of our expertise or this book. However, it is intriguing to note that in each of the traditions there is clear convergence of agreement on these universal concerns and behaviors, as well as the effect appropriate to the morally educated and ethically acting individual.

3. THE ETHICS OF BUSINESS AND THE MORAL MANAGER

What Is Business Ethics?

There may be a very simple answer to this question: each of us lives within and abides by the rules, the laws, etc. But much of what is written today informs us that this simple approach is just not enough—compliance with the laws and rules does not cover the complexity of issues and dilemmas that face the moral and ethical manager. Thankfully, we have child labor laws, privacy laws, and regulations from the

Occupational Safety & Health Administration that help protect us, but are they enough to keep our ethics and integrity intact on issues not regulated?

Ethics has been a topic for philosophers for more than 2,500 years. Today it is a subject for shareholders, employers, boards of directors, employees, management, the media, etc. It claims much attention in the press as things go awry within organizations. A great deal of pension reform is currently "on the table" as a result of the Enron debacle. In light of what happened to all Enron's shareholders, would the definition of business ethics as "the norms that a community defines and institutionalizes to prevent individuals from pursuing self-interest at the expense of others" hold up? (Dalla Costa, p. 71)

Michael Daigneault, ERC president, posits business ethics exist in "an organization that includes standards of conduct such as honesty, fairness, responsibility and trust." In *Good Intentions Aside*, Laura Nash takes us further:

> Working from nearly two hundred corporate ethics codes gathered by the Business Roundtable, interviews with literally thousands of executives, and drawing on pro- and anti-business articles in the general press, I would suggest that the generally same standards of decency drive our society's definitions of business integrity. Thus a general description of business integrity would comprise the following basic values:
>
> *Honesty*—accuracy in assessing and representing the business and any activity relevant to a business.

Reliability—being consistent in action with one's purported values. This can imply anything from consistently living up to product claims to not punishing employees who live out the standards that you claim are integral to the business.

Fairness—balancing the rights of various constituencies with consistency and goodwill. While companies differ strongly in terms of how far they will carry their sense of stakeholder responsibility in noncommercial relationships, there seems to be more agreement over the commercial manifestations of the ethic: fairness means adopting neither a totally buyer-beware nor seller-beware ethic. Rather than assume exclusive responsibility for every unforeseen outcome of a transaction, the seller accepts responsibility for keeping the specific promises that are made or implied to customers and employees.

Pragmatism—making concrete contributions to the ongoing financial and organizational health of the business.

These four hallmarks of business integrity cover a wealth of ethical issues in a commonsense way. The first three preclude deception, intentional injury, favoritism, conflict of interest, and the abrogation of responsibility to pay for mistakes. The last precludes all forms of white-collar crime, inefficiency, and waste…. Most important, *integrity is a condition that demands that you walk as you talk.*" (p. 33)

The Moral Manager

It seems to us that we can all agree that much more is involved in business ethics than merely having a written code of ethical conduct. Just ask the employees.

Managerial Ethics

According to an article, "Turn Employees into Saints?" by Susan J. Wells in *HR Magazine*, December 1999, many businesses

> have taken no more than an initial step in addressing ethics issues. Seventy-three percent of 747 HR professionals say their organizations have developed written standards or codes of ethical business conduct.... However, 61 percent of respondents said their companies don't provide training on ethical standards. And only 31 percent said their organizations have ethics offices or ombudsmen.

One of the most important aspects of managerial ethics is "walk as you talk." A written standard or code is NOT enough. Beyond establishing a code of ethical conduct, it is imperative to include integrity and ethics in the company's vision/mission statement. A company's vision/mission statement, its values, its goals—all tell a story, and one hopes that story is compelling and inspiring. Typically, organizations create a vision/mission as a vehicle for communicating to all of its constituencies what is important—it provides direction as to the organization's destiny. Managers can use it as a guide in decision-making, hiring, motivating, etc. It helps to ensure that the people hired have values and beliefs that match those that are held by the leaders and managers; it can help to create a sense of teamwork and commitment; and can help to increase the organization's chances for success.

It is also important to communicate to employees that we recognize business ethics often means dealing with issues where there is no clear indication of what is right and what is wrong. Believing in the innate goodness of human beings, we can easily convince ourselves in a case of right versus wrong, the high road will be taken by most, and the right course of action followed. It's not always that straightforward, however.

According to Rushworth Kidder in *How Good People Make Tough Choices: Resolving the Dilemmas of Ethical Living*:

> The **really** tough choices, then, don't center upon right versus wrong. They involve right versus right. They are genuine dilemmas precisely because each side is firmly rooted in one of our basic, core values. Four such dilemmas are so common to our experience that they stand as models, patterns, or paradigms.
>
> They are:
> Truth versus loyalty
> Individual versus community
> Short-term versus long-term
> Justice versus mercy
>
> …How does this process of determining a paradigm help us make tough choices? I think it works in three ways:
>
> - It helps us cut through mystery, complexity, and confusion—assuring us that, however elaborate and multifaceted, dilemmas can be reduced to common patterns. By doing so, it reminds us that **this** dilemma—the one that

just landed on my desk in the middle of an otherwise ordinary Tuesday afternoon—is not some unique event created *sui generis* out of thin air and never before having happened to anyone in the universe. It is, instead, an ultimately manageable problem, bearing strong resemblance to lots of other problems and quite amenable to analysis.

- It helps us strip away extraneous detail and get to the heart of the matter. Under this sort of analysis, the fundamental fact that makes this an authentic dilemma—the clashing of core moral values—stands out in bold relief. Looking at this clash, we can easily see why we have a conflict: Each value is right, and each appears to exclude the other.
- It helps us separate right-versus-wrong from right-versus-right. The more we work with true ethical dilemmas, the more we realize that they fit rather naturally into these paradigms. So any situation that fits one or more of the paradigms must in fact be an issue of right versus right.

This is a "roadmap" that can be extremely useful to managers facing ethical problems in the workplace. And if this "roadmap" is promulgated throughout the organization, it will provide a foundation and a common language for use with others for discussion of these tough issues.

Characteristics of an Ethical Organization

There are many traits and characteristics we might name here. One of the most comprehensive overviews of a principled/ethical organization has been published by The Caux Round Table (CRT), a group of senior business leaders from Europe, Japan, and North America who are committed to the promotion of principled business leadership. They believe that business has a crucial role in identifying and promoting sustainable and equitable solutions to key global issues affecting the physical, social and economic environments.

<u>Caux Round Table Stakeholder Principles</u>

<u>Customers:</u> Treat all customers with dignity, irrespective of whether they purchase our products and services directly from us or otherwise acquire them in the market. Therefore, we have a responsibility to:

- Provide our customers with the highest quality products and services consistent with their requirements
- Treat our customers fairly in all aspects of our business transactions, including a high level of service and remedies for their dissatisfaction
- Make every effort to ensure that the health and safety of our customers, as well as the quality of their environment, will be sustained or enhanced by our products and service
- Assure respect for human dignity in products offered, marketing, and advertising, and
- Respect the integrity of the culture of our customers

The Moral Manager

<u>Employees:</u> We believe in the dignity of every employee and in taking employee interests seriously. We therefore have a responsibility to:

- Provide jobs and compensation that improve workers' living conditions
- Provide working conditions that respect each employee's health and dignity
- Be honest in communications with employees and open in sharing information, limited only by legal and competitive constraints
- Listen to, and where possible, act on employee suggestions, ideas, requests, and complaints
- Engage in good faith negotiations when conflict arises
- Avoid discriminatory practices and guarantee equal treatment and opportunity in areas such as gender, age, race and religion
- Promote in the business itself the employment of differently abled people in places of work where they can be genuinely useful
- Protect employees from avoidable injury and illness in the workplace
- Encourage and assist employees in developing relevant and transferable skills and knowledge, and
- Be sensitive to the serious unemployment problems frequently associated with business decision, and work with governments, employee groups, other agencies and each other in addressing these dislocations.

Owners/Investors: We believe in honoring the trust our investors place in us. We therefore have a responsibility to:

- Apply professional and diligent management in order to secure a fair and competitive return on our owners' investment
- Disclose relevant information to owner/investors subject only to legal requirements and competitive constraints
- Conserve, protect and increase the owners/investors' assets, and
- Respect owner/investors' requests, suggestions, complaints, and formal resolutions.

Suppliers: Our relationship with suppliers and subcontractors must be based on mutual respect. We therefore have a responsibility to:

- Seek fairness and truthfulness in all our activities, including pricing, licensing, and rights to sell
- Ensure that our business activities are free from coercion and unnecessary litigation
- Foster long-term stability in the supplier relationship in return for value, quality, competitiveness and reliability
- Share information with suppliers and integrate them into our planning processes
- Pay suppliers on time and in accordance with agreed terms of trade, and
- Seek, encourage and prefer suppliers and subcontractors whose employment practices respect human dignity.

The Moral Manager

Competitors: We believe that fair economic competition is one of the basic requirements for increasing the wealth of nations and ultimately for making possible the just distribution of goods and services. We therefore have a responsibility to:

- Foster open markets for trade and investment
- Promote competitive behavior that is socially and environmentally beneficial and demonstrates mutual respect among competitors
- Refrain from either seeking or participating in questionable payments or favors to secure competitive advantages
- Respect both tangible and intellectual property rights, and
- Refuse to acquire commercial information by dishonest or unethical means, such as industrial espionage.

Communities: We believe that as global corporate citizens we can contribute to such forces of reform and human rights as we are at work in the communities in which we operate. We therefore have a responsibility in the communities to:

- Support peace, security, diversity and social integration
- Respect the integrity of local cultures, and
- Be a good corporate citizen through charitable donations, educational and cultural contributions, and employee participation in community and civic affairs.

Universal Moral and Ethical Education

This should provide significant guidance as to the characteristics and behaviors indigenous to ethical organizations. At a minimum, an ethical organization's characteristics must encompass dignity, trust, and respect; openness in sharing information; honesty in communications; building strong partnerships and communities; listening to our constituencies and acting on ideas, complaints, etc.; providing customers with high quality products and services consistent with their requirements; and fairness and integrity in all dealings.

Benefits of Managing Ethics in the Workplace

What happens to an organization today that is deemed unethical in its practices? We can take a look at the plummeting stock prices of those companies whose accounting practices are questioned or where it becomes public that child labor is used in the manufacture of their products, etc. Enron's reputation is in shreds, and its accounting firm, Arthur Andersen, has already experienced a significant loss in its client roster. Thus, not only does questionable conduct result in a loss of credibility, trust, and support in the short-term, but it can definitely also lead to a loss of profitability in the long-term.

Dalla Costa tells us that business benefits from an ethical orientation, because: (p. 204)

- An ethical corporate character wins trust
- A trusted company earns greater loyalty from customers.

- A trusted company attracts and holds on to trusting people.
- A trusted company attracts responsible strategic partners.
- A trusting work environment creates the support that fuels creativity.
- A trusting work environment is faster and more responsive.
- A trusting environment is more open to change.
- A trusting company is motivated to produce excellence in both revenues and social results.
- A trusting company creates personal growth opportunities for its people.

People want to work in environments that are purposeful and successful and in which they can continue to grow and develop professionally and personally. Ethical organizations provide such an environment and become "magnets" for people with similar values, ethics and goals. The people who are drawn to these organizations, in turn, create greater value for the organization.

If an organization has a reputation for being trustworthy and ethical, its public image is enhanced. And a positive public image can mean an increase in those willing to invest in the company.

How to Manage Ethics in the Workplace

The most important point here is not to be an organization that has an ethics program, but most of the employees

Universal Moral and Ethical Education

don't know it or to be an organization that has a written policy or code, but none of the supporting programs. It is important to develop and communicate policies and practices in keeping with the code of ethics and to train the members of the organization, so everyone is clear about the importance of ethics in the workplace.

*An organization that has an ethics program about which none of its employees are aware, or a written code of ethics, but without supporting programs, cannot expect significant results from this program or policy. *

In *Beyond Integrity: A Judeo-Christian Approach to Business Ethics*, Rae and Wong provide a moral decision-making model (p. 639):

1. **Gather the facts**. Frequently, ethical dilemmas can be resolved simply by clarifying the facts of the case in question. In those cases that prove to be more difficult, gathering the facts is the essential first step prior to any ethical analysis and reflection on the case. In analyzing a case, we want to know the available facts at hand as well as any facts currently not known but that need to be ascertained. Thus one is asking not only "What do you know?" but also "What do we need to know?" in order to make an intelligent ethical decision.

2. **Determine the ethical issues**. The ethical issues are stated in terms of competing interests or goods. It's these conflicting interests that actually make for an ethical dilemma. The issues should be presented in a _____ versus _____ format in order to reflect the interests that are colliding in a particular ethical

dilemma. For example, in business ethics there is often a conflict between the right of a firm to make a fair profit and its obligation to the community.

3. What principles have a bearing on the case? In any ethical dilemma, there are certain moral values or principles that are central to the conflicting positions being taken. It is critical to identify these principles, and in some cases, to determine whether some principles are to be weighted more heavily than others. Clearly, biblical principles will be weighted the most heavily. There may be other principles that speak to the case that come from other sources. There may be constitutional principles or principles drawn from natural law that supplement the biblical principles that come into play here. The principles that come out of your sense of mission and calling are also important to consider.

4. List the alternatives. Part of the creative thinking involved in resolving an ethical dilemma involves coming up with various alternative courses of action. Although there will be some alternatives that you will rule out without much thought, in general the more alternatives that are listed, the better the chance that your list will include some high-quality ones. In addition, you may come up with some very creative alternatives that you had not considered before.

5. Compare the alternatives with the principles. At this point, the task is one of eliminating alternatives according to the moral principles that have a bearing on the case. In many instances, the case will be resolved at this point, since the principles will eliminate all alternatives except one. In fact, the purpose of this comparison is to see if there is a clear decision that can be made without further deliberation. If a clear decision is not forthcoming, then the next part of the model must be considered. At the least, some of the alternatives may be eliminated by this step of comparison.

6. **Weigh the consequences.** If the principles do not yield a clear decision, then a consideration of the consequences of the remaining available alternatives is in order. Both positive and negative consequences are to be considered. They should be informally weighed, since some positive consequences are more beneficial than others and some negative consequences are more detrimental than others.

7. **Make a decision.** Deliberation cannot go on forever. At some point, a decision must be made. Realize that one common element in ethical dilemmas is that there are no easy and painless solutions to them. Frequently the decision that is made is one that involves the least number of problems or negative consequences, not one that is devoid of them.

To truly manage ethics in the workplace, be sure there are tools such as the moral decision-making model available to employees, and that they are trained in how to use them. Case studies are a very effective way of allowing employees to practice utilizing the model, and should create a "safe" environment for discussing the rigors of ethical decision-making.

Guidelines for a Manager

Talk the talk, walk the walk, walk the talk. You must set a good example for others to follow. There is no credibility for managers who do not do what they say they will do. There is no integrity in expecting others to behave and perform in ways management would not. We must build and engender trust in our organizations.

Here are the 12 Building Blocks of Trust (from http://www.ethics.org/etideas.html):

- Be direct
- Be inclusive
- Be candid
- Avoid blaming
- Listen intently
- Remain accessible
- Act with integrity
- Be accountable
- Keep promises
- Share praise
- Value diversity

Universal Moral and Ethical Education

It is also important to understand your own ethical style and that of those with whom you work. As part of an ethics program, work should be done on identifying and understanding the different approaches to ethical behavior. Robert C. Solomon in *A Better Way to Think about Business* provides us with seven ethical systems (page 117):

1. RULE-BOUND: thinking and acting on the basis of rules and principles, with only secondary regard to circumstances or possible exceptions.
2. UTILITARIAN: weighing probably consequences, both to the company or the profession and to the public well-being. Principles are more important only as rules of thumb. "The greatest good for the greatest number of people" is the ultimate test for any action or decision.
3. PROFESSIONAL: evaluating all decisions first in terms of benefit to the profession, the institution, and the company and its reputation.
4. LOYALIST: duties and obligations defined by way of identification with the company or the organization. In business, "the company man."
5. VIRTUOUS: every action is measured in terms of its reflection on one's character (or the profession, institution, or company reputation) without immediate regard to consequences and often without paying much attention to general principles.
6. INTUITIVE: making decisions on the basis of conscience, even without deliberation, argument, or reasons. Intuitive thinkers tend to be impatient with more deliberative deontological and utilitarian types.
7. EMPATHETIC: following one's feelings of sympathy

and compassion. "Putting oneself in the other's place" is the modus operandi of the empathetic style, whether the "other" be a competitor ("How would we like it if he...") or a client ("I can easily imagine how it would feel to be...")

In *It's Good Business: Ethics and Free Enterprise for the New Millennium*, Solomon provides us with eight crucial rules for ethical thinking in business:

Rule No. 1: Consider the well-being of others, including the well-being of nonparticipants.
Rule No. 2: Think as a member of the business community, not as an isolated individual.
Rule No. 3: Obey, but do not depend solely on, the law.
Rule No. 4: Think of yourself—and your company—as part of society, not just "the market."
Rule No. 5: Obey moral rules.
Rule No. 6: Think "objectively."
Rule No. 7: Ask the question, "What sort of person would do such a thing?"
Rule No. 8: Respect the customs and beliefs of others, but not at the expense of your own ethics.

Rae and Wong would like us to keep in mind (p. 608-609):

- There is no single ideal approach to corporate ethics.

Universal Moral and Ethical Education

- Top management must be committed.
- Developing a structure is not sufficient by itself.
- Raising the ethical consciousness of an organization is not easy.

Raising the ethical consciousness of our organizations may not be easy, but it must be considered worth the effort. Creating an environment of trust, so people are comfortable coming forward with concerns and issues of a moral and ethical nature is a must, as is implementing the policies, programs, and practices necessary to support it.

Roles and Responsibilities of a Manager

It should be obvious by now that the involvement and support of the organization's chief executive is mandatory in establishing an ethics program within the organization. Employees will know if he/she is not fully aware of, involved in, and supportive of such a program. He/she should be involved in its development, should play a major role in announcing it, and be known as the driving force behind it. It may also be useful to formulate an ethics committee at either the Board or senior management level or both. This puts some "teeth" into the program – the message goes out that time and talent are being invested in this important effort. Many organizations today are creating a role of ombudsperson; this position helps to institutionalize moral and ethical values in the workplace.

You may want to consider the following list of potential participants in drafting the code of ethics and in designing supporting programs: the general counsel, the CEO, senior human resources executive(s), the Chairman, senior financial executive(s), the board of directors, senior public affairs/investor relations executive(s), senior marketing executive(s), senior manufacturing executive(s), employee representatives, senior sales executive(s), senior purchasing executive(s), consultants, the founder or member of the founder's family, and randomly selected employees.

What being a manager comes down to, argues Shapiro, "is a willingness to make decisions, think through the implications, live with the consequences, and learn from mistakes and keep going." (Seglin, p. 184)

If you make a mistake, admit it. Have conviction and act with integrity.

Tips for Managers on Establishing an Ethical Business

Nancy Croft Baker, in her article, "Heightened Interest in Ethics Education Reflects Employer, Employee Concerns," advises us first and foremost to "establish a code of responsible business conduct." It is highly recommended that employees be part of the process of developing the code. The code itself will help provide a guide for employees in the way the organization expects them to conduct themselves as representatives of the organization and employee participation in its development helps to ensure their "buy-in." The next step is to disseminate the code and "require employees to verify that they have read and understand the code." This adds their integrity and credibility to the process. To truly get employees to understand that the code is taken very seriously by the organization, it is imperative to "integrate ethics into performance evaluations." Making ethics part of this process indicates to managers that their performance in this critical area is observed and measured. It provides the opportunity to discuss how their ethical behavior (or lack thereof) is impacting others in the organization and what needs to be done to enhance or correct the performance in this crucial area. The organization **must** "recognize and reward ethical behavior." We are all aware of the effectiveness of reinforcements. If we want a behavior to be repeated, we must acknowledge the individuals who exhibit that behavior and provide a reward as reinforcement. Doing so will definitely help make the behavior become routine. "Establish an ethics hot line or advisory service." This gives employees the opportunity to communicate expediently with "authorities" within the organization on ethical issues and/or bring questionable conduct to light. "Incorporate ethics questions in employee opinion surveys." If ethics does not appear in these surveys, it undermines the entire validity of the program. If it has importance in and to the organization, and if employees may have an opinion about the program, it belongs in the survey. We also need to keep the entire topic "fresh" for employees through training workshops, brainstorming sessions, ethics videos, case studies, etc.

Creating Your Own Ethical Policy

Company ethics statements or codes may contain a wide variety of topics. We provide a list here of those most often addressed from The Conference Board's *Corporate Ethics Practices*, 1992:

- Fundamental guiding principles of the company
- Purchasing
- Proprietary information
- Workplace safety
- Environmental responsibility
- Marketing
- Intellectual property
- Confidentiality of employee records
- Product safety
- Employee privacy
- Drug-related issues
- Technological innovation
- AIDS

Effective ethics programs distinguish between the ethical and the legal, must be endorsed by top management, must involve employees from the beginning, and must recognize that ethical problems are everywhere.

The Caux Round Table, in addition to the Stakeholder Principles noted earlier, has put information together that they hope will provide a world standard against which business behavior can be measured (from http://astro.temple.edu/~dialogue/Codes/caux.htm). In so doing, they hope that a process will begin that identifies shared values, reconciles differing values, and thereby develops a shared perspective on business behavior acceptable to and honored by all. Their General Principles for business include:

Principle 1. The responsibilities of business: beyond shareholders, toward stakeholders.
The value of a business to society is the wealth and

employment it creates and the marketable products and services it provides to consumers at a reasonable price commensurate with quality. To create such value, a business must maintain its own economic health and viability, but survival is not a sufficient goal.

Businesses have a role to play in improving the lives of their customers, employees, and shareholders by sharing with them the wealth they have created. Suppliers and competitors as well should expect businesses to honor their obligations in a spirit of honesty and fairness. As responsible citizens of the local, national, regional and global communities in which they operate, businesses share a part in shaping the future of those communities.

Principle 2. The economic and social impact of business: toward innovation, justice and world community.

Businesses established in foreign countries to develop, produce or sell should also contribute to the social advancement of those countries by creating productive employment and helping to raise the purchasing power of their citizens. Businesses also should contribute to human rights, education, welfare, and vitalization of the countries in which they operate.

Businesses should contribute to economic and social development not only in the countries in which they operate, but also in the world community at large, through effective and prudent use of resources, free and fair competition, and emphasis upon innovation in technology, production methods, marketing and communications.

Principle 3. Business behavior: beyond the letter of law, toward a spirit of trust.
While accepting the legitimacy of trade secrets, businesses should recognize that sincerity, candor, truthfulness, the keeping of promises, and transparency contribute not only to their own credibility and stability but also to the smoothness and efficiency of business transactions, particularly on the international level.

Principle 4. Respect for rules.
To avoid trade frictions and to promote freer trade-equal conditions for competition, and fair and equitable treatment for all participants, businesses should respect international and domestic rules. In addition, they should recognize that some behavior, although legal, might still have adverse consequences.

Principle 5. Support for multilateral trade.
Business should support the multilateral trade systems of the GATT/World Trade Organization and similar international agreements. They should cooperate in efforts to promote the progressive and judicious liberalization of trade and to relax those domestic measures that unreasonably hinder global commerce, while giving due respect to national policy objectives.

Principle 6. Respect for the environment.
A business should protect, and, where possible, improve the environment, promote sustainable development, and prevent the wasteful use of natural resources.

Principle 7. Avoidance of illicit operations.
A business should not participate in or condone bribery, money laundering, or other corrupt practices: indeed, it should seek cooperation with others to eliminate them. It should not trade in arms or other materials used for terrorist activities, drug traffic or other organized crime.

Treating People Well Brings Its Own Rewards

We are all familiar with the Golden Rule: "Do unto others as you would have them do unto you": treat others as we would like to be treated. The Platinum Rule encourages us to treat others as they wish to be treated. We should become intimately familiar with the Platinum Rule and put it into daily practice.

If employees do not feel valued within the organization, typically they will exit at the first opportunity. Turnover can be extremely costly to a business; there are significant administrative costs involved in replacing an employee, in addition to the loss of empirical knowledge and the lack of return of investment on training and developing the individual. The fact that the organization (and the organization means managers) does not treat its people well becomes public knowledge, and we are no longer able to hire the talent, the human resources, needed for the business to achieve its goals.

In today's business world, it is just too costly not to treat people well. And, it is the right and ethical thing to do.

Implementation Steps

Dalla Costa provides us with an Implementation Plan for an Ethical Organization in his book *The Ethical Imperative*:

Process	Involving
Unlearning	What are the biases impeding an ethical orientation? Which behaviors risk or undermine ethical virtue? What systems, traditions or assumptions support these? What is the critical ethical inadequacy? Or risk?
Management	How have the board and CEO signaled ethical expectations?
Responsibility	Which behaviors by example reinforce or undermine that ethic? How has an ethical orientation been integrated with strategy? How is senior management accountable for ethical performance? How are shareholders engaged in the issues and decisions regarding an ethical orientation?
Employee	In what ways is an ethical orientation included in performance appraisals and labor agreements?

Universal Moral and Ethical Education

Contract	How is ethical orientation expressed in recruiting and hiring? Which reciprocities does the company use to model ethical behavior for employees? Do all individuals in the company understand the ethical orientation and their responsibility for compliance? Would all employees similarly and accurately reflect back the values, expectations and processes for an ethical orientation?
Strat-Ethic Plan	How has the company expressed its commitment to a global ethic? What are the temptations and critical ethical factors to be focused on? What are the company's critical virtues to develop and exercise? What is the shape and scope of the company's ethical orientation model? • What are the process steps for understanding ethical implications and acting ethically? • What are the internal and external guides for ethical interaction? • What are the steps for engaging team members and management

in ethical deliberation and decisions?
- What resources are available for ethical understanding, disagreements and resolutions?
- What is the process for managing ethical breakdowns?
  - For problem acknowledgment?
  - For addressing the issue?
  - For absorbing the learning?
  - For sharing and institutionalizing the lesson?
  - For rewarding those who acted ethically?

Ethical Orientation Audits	What are the internal measures of success for an ethical orientation? What are the external measures? How are these benchmarked and continuously improved? Are these formalized in the company's annual report? How are lessons and results shared with employees? How are behaviors reinforced or discouraged? In what ways does the reward and compensation structure encourage an ethical orientation? What are the steps for encoding new learning?

Updating How are all employees stretched and strengthened in their ethical orientation?
What new issues require a deepening ethical maturity?

Provide education, leadership, accountability, organizational systems and decision processes, auditing and controls, penalties/consequences and rewards.

Communicate, communicate, communicate.

Train, train, train.

Lead by example.

CONCLUSION

Businesses are beginning to understand that they play a role in a larger context. That process can be continued only by the managers in those businesses. The British trade association, RSA, has stated: "Tomorrow's company is managed by people who can hold collaboration and competition in their heads at the same time, and see the company's identity as including all stakeholders. Yesterday's companies are managed by people who see only themselves and their immediate colleagues as *us*, and everyone else as them." (Dalla Costa, p. 218)

The making of a moral manager is a complex and conflicted process. That process must begin with the understanding that this idea of inclusion, the *us*, may mean the entire population of planet Earth. It is a frighteningly sobering thought, but it provides the context for the difficult ethical dilemmas managers face.

The manager occasionally must choose between a moral, ethical action and an immoral, yet possibly easier action proposed by upper management. As you've seen in this chapter, there are many ethical guidelines to follow; yet they all have something in common — there must be a determination of what is right and what right actions should be taken. As we've witnessed through history, the right choice can be extremely difficult to make and take considerable courage. The concept of right versus right should prove very helpful in the ethical education of managers; it will help them to understand why some of these issues are so difficult to resolve. Employees are the people who represent and provide value to the enterprise. Customers are the purchasers of that value. Neither is shackled to one company, therefore logic dictates that it is better not to cheat, steal from or lie to these individual groups.

Yet, there will always be dilemmas. The customer may always be right—but not if he or she is in a drunken rage on an airliner in mid-flight. A customer's business is a company's lifeblood—but not if the customer is demanding a large kickback as the price of doing business. Employees are valued members of the company family, but they have to follow the rules set for their safety and productivity. A moral manager in an ethical company should not tolerate drug use, sexual harassment, absenteeism, or poor performance. There should be **no** exceptions. If a senior vice president does not wear the appropriate personal protective equipment to ensure his or her safety, he or she should be dismissed as quickly as would be a line worker.

We recognize that all this is easier said than done. It is, however, our firm hope that some of what has been presented here strikes a chord, and sets you and your organization in motion toward establishing a set of guidelines to help managers take appropriate and moral actions.

REFERENCES

Alasuutari, P. (1997). *Researching culture: Qualitative method and cultural studies.* London: Sage.

Beauchamp, T. L. and Bowie, N. E., eds. (1983). *Ethical theory and business.* 2nd ed. Englewood Cliffs, NJ: Prentice-Hall.

Beekun, R. (1996). "Islamic business ethics." Available on line at http://www.islamist.org/ethicshm.pdf

Berenbeim, Ronald E. (1992). "Corporate Ethics Practices." New York: The Conference Board.

Breitowitz, Y. "Jewish business ethics: An introductory perspective." *Jewish Law.* Available on line at http://www.jlaw.com/Articles/JewBusEthI.html

Brenner, S. (1992). *Journal of Business Ethics* 11: 391-399.

"Business ethics, ethics training." Available on line at http://www.bsr.org/resourcecenter/

Caux Round Table. "The Principles for Business." Available online at http://www.cauxroundtable.org/English/htm

Complete guide to ethics management: An ethics toolkit for managers. Available on line at http://www.mapnp.org/library/ethics/ethxgde.htm

Crane Andrew. (1999). "Are you ethical? Please tick Yes or No: On researching ethics in business organizations," *Journal of Business Ethics* 20: 237-248.

Daigneault, M. G. (1999). "Compliance to ethics to integrity." *Ethics Today* (Spring). Available on line at http://www.ethics.org/etcomm.html
Dalla Costa, John. (1998). *The Ethical Imperative: Why Moral Leadership Is Good Business.* Reading, Massachusetts: Perseus Books.
De George, R. T. (1991a). "Will success spoil business ethics?" In *Business ethics: The state of the art*, ed. R. Edward Freeman, pp. 42-56. New York: Oxford University Press.
_____. (1991b). "On economic and ethical value." Institute for Business and Professional Ethics, Available on line at http://www.depaul.edu/ethics/evalue.html
_____. (1999). "Business ethics and the information age." *Business & Society Review* 104 (3) (Fall): 261-278.
_____. (1990). *Business Ethics.* 3rd ed. New York: Macmillan.
_____. (2000). "Ethics in international business, a contradiction in terms." *Business Credit* 102 (8) (Sept): 50-52.
Donaldson, J. (1989). *Key issues in business ethics.* London: Academic Press.
Donaldson, J. and Davis, P. (1990). "Business ethics." *Management Decision* 28 (6).
Dougherty, T. C. (1999). "Building trust in the workplace." *Ethics Today* (Winter). Available on line at http://www.ethics.org/etideas.html
Freeman, R. E. and Gilbert, Jr. D. R. (1987). *Corporate Strategy and the Search for Ethics.* Englewood Cliffs, NJ: Prentice-Hall.
Green, Ronald M. (1995). *The ethical manager: A new method of business ethics.* New York: Macmillan.
Greenspan, A. (1999). Commencement address at Harvard University, Cambridge, Massachusetts, June 10, 1999. Available on line at http://www.federalreserve.gov/boarddocs/speeches/1999/199906102.htm

Guy, M.E. (1990). *Ethical decision-making in everyday work situations*. Westport, Connecticut: Greenwood Press, Quorum Books.

Harvey B., ed. (1994). *Business ethics: A European approach*. London: Prentice Hall.

Hoffman, W.M. and Frederick, R.E. (1995). *Business ethics: Readings and cases in corporate morality*. 3rd ed. New York: McGraw-Hill.

Kidder, Rushworth M. (1995). *How good people make tough choices: Resolving the dilemmas of ethical living*. New York: William Morrow and Company.

Lewis, J. "Doing the right things." Available on line at http://www.kcsmallbiz.com/old/9709/p10.html

Madsen, P. and Shafritz, J. M. (1990). *Essentials of business ethics*. 11(63): 29.

McHugh, F. P. and Natale, S. M. (1992). *Things old and new: Catholic social teaching revisited*. Von Hugel Institute, St. Edmund College, Cambridge University; Lanham, MD: University Press of America.

Mc Namara, C. (1996). "Eight guidelines to manage ethics in the work place." Available on line at http://www.mapnp.org/library/ethics/ethxgde.htm#anchor39675

Mc Namara, C. (1996a). "Six key roles and responsibilities in ethics management." Available on line at http://www.mapnp.org/library/ethics/ethxgde.htm#anchor41892

_____. (1996b). "Ten benefits of business ethics." *Complete guide to ethics management*, Available on line at http://www.mapnp.org/library/ethics/ethxgde.htm#anchor33077

Mc Shulskis, E. (1997). "Job stress can prompt unethical behavior." *HR Magazine* 42 (7) (July): 22-23.

Nash, L. L. (1990). *Good intentions aside: A manager's guide to resolving ethical problems*. Boston: Harvard Business School Press.

Natale, S. M. (1983). *Ethics and morals in business*. Birmingham, Alabama: REP.

———. (1987). *Ethics and morals in business*. 2nd ed. Birmingham, Alabama: REP.

———, ed. (1989). *Ethics, morals and conflict in industry*. Lanham, MD: University Press of America.

———, ed. (2000). *Business, education and training: A value-laden process. Vol. 7: New wine in old bottles*. Oxford University Centre for the Study of Values in Education and Business (OXSVEB). Lanham, MD: University Press of America.

——— and Fenton, M.B., eds. (1997). *Business education and training: A value-laden process. Vol. 2: Education and value conflicts: The developing professional*. Oxford University Centre for the Study of Values in Education and Business (OXSVEB). Lanham, MD: University Press of America.

———, Hoffman, R. and Hayward, G., eds. (1998). *Corporate structures, business and the management of values*. Lanham, MD: University Press of America.

———, Libertella, A.F. and Hayward, G. (2001). *Higher education in crisis: The corporate eclipse of the university*. Binghamton, NY: Global Publications, Binghamton University, SUNY.

——— and Rothschild, B. M., eds. (1995). *Values, work, education: The meaning of work* (vol. 1), Studies in Social Values Series. Amsterdam, Netherlands; Atlanta, GA: Rodolfi Press.

——— and Wilson, J. B. (1991). *Central issues in moral and ethical education* . Oxford Philosophy Trust; Lanham, MD: University Press of America.

Navran, F. (1996). The Ethic's Resource Center's desktop guide to total ethics management. Available on line at http://www.ethics.org/articles/arole.html

Pastin, M. (1986). *The hard problems of management: Gaining the ethics edge*. San Francisco: Jossey-Bass. Available on line at http://www.JosseyBass.com/catalog

Rae, S. B. and Wong, K. L. (1996). *Beyond integrity: A Judeo-Christian approach to business ethics*. Michigan: Zondervan Publishing House.

Reidenbach, R. E. and Robin, D. P. (1990). "Toward the development of a multidimensional scale for improving evaluations of business ethics." *Journal of Business Ethics*, 9: 639-653.

Seglin, J. L. (2000). *The Good, the bad, and your business: Choosing Right when ethical dilemmas pull you apart*. New York: Wiley and Sons, Inc.

Solomon, R. C. (1997). *A better way to think about business: How personal integrity leads to corporate success*. New York: Oxford University Press.

_____. (1999). *It's good business: Ethics and free enterprise for the new millennium*. Maryland: Rowman & Littlefield Publishers, Inc.

"Tips on establishing an ethical business." Available on line at http://www.bbb.org/library/ethical.asp

Tsalikis, J. and Nwachukwu, O. (1988). "Cross-cultural business ethics: Ethical belief differences between Blacks and Whites." *Journal of Business Ethics*, 7: 745-754.

_____ and Ortiz-Buonafina, M. (1990). "Ethical beliefs: differences of males and females". *Journal of Business Ethics*, 9: 509-517.

Velasquez, M. G. (1982). *Business ethics: Concepts and cases*. Englewood Cliffs, NJ: Prentice Hall.

Wallace, D. (1986). "One description of highly ethical organization." Available on line at http://www.mapnp.org/library/ethics/ethxgde.htm#anchor35028

Wells, S. J. (1999). "Turn Employees into Saints?" *HR Magazine* (Dec.):
White, J. (1978). *Honesty, morality and conscience.* (Colorado Springs, CO: NavPress).
Zeidman, B. (1998). "Corporate social responsibility: Beyond traditional ethics programs." *Ethics Today* (Winter).

Other useful sites:
www.shrm.org/diversity/definingdiversity.htm
www.bsr.org/resourcecenter
http://ecampus.bentley.edu/debt.cbe/survey.html
http://astro.temple.edu/~dialogue/codes/cmj_codes.htm
http://ecampus.bentley.edu/debt/cbe/meoprog.htm
http://ecampus.bentley.edu/debt/cbe/syllabus1htm
www.ethics.org/etcomn.html
www.ethic.org/etideas.html
http://personal2.stthomas.edu/gwschlabach/docs/econjust.htm
http://216.46.241.4/about/entries.asp
www.netcheck.com/nytimes.htm
www.ethics.org/etideas.html
www.cnn.com/TECH/computing/9906/22/ethics.ent.idg/index.html
http://www.aaas.org/spp/welcome.htm
http://www.aeu.org/concept_map.html
www.ethics.org/training/environment.htmhttp://www.depaul.edu/ethics/montana.html
http://www.depaul.edu/ethics/montana.html
http://www.uncc.edu/ragiacal/ethframes.html
http://www.business-ethics.com
http://cgi.exp.com/reqauth/user_invoice.cgi?inv_id=77089
http://www.altpress.org
BizEthics@aol.com

http://www.exp.com
http://www.islamist.org/ethics.html
http://www.businessethics.ca/articles.html
http://www.mapnp.org/library/ethics/ethxgde.htm
http://www.islamist.org/News.pdf
http://www.jlaw.com/Articles/psharah1.html

Index

A

A Better Way to Think about Business, 149
absence of trust, 34
acceptance, 35
accepted conduct, 81
accountability, 161
acting out their feelings, 59
action, 69
adjustments, 86
agape, 69
aggression, 17
alienation, 33
applied moral education, 126
approaches to ethical behavior, 149
Aristotle, 92
assessment, 120
Attila the Hun, 91
auditing and controls, 161
authoritarian personality, 14
authoritarian teacher, 41
authoritarianism, 19, 20
and chaos, 20
authority, 9, 14, 36
autonomy, 12, 14, 38
avoidance of illicit operations, 157

B

Baha'ism, 125
Baker, Nancy Croft, 152
balancing ethical dilemmas, 100
Beekun, Dr. Rafik , 132
behavior, 56, 75
patterns, 56
behaviors by example, 158
beliefs, 124, 136
Beyond Integrity: A Judeo-Christian Approach to Business Ethics, 145
biases, 158
biblical principles, 146
"big picture", 4
Breitowitz, Rabbi Yitzchok , 128

INDEX

bribery, 157
Buddhism, 125
building strong partnerships and communities, 143
business
    behavior, 154, 156
    conduct, 103
    ethics, 43, 44, 50, 129, 130, 134, 137, 146
    integrity, 134, 135
business' decision makers, 7
buying influence or engaging in conflict of interest, 97

C

capitalism, 4, 49
care-based thinking, 113
categories of ethical dilemmas, 96
categorization, 54
Caux Round Table, 139, 154
characteristics, 138
Christian approach, 130, 131
"Class War", 21
classical business management structures, 4
classification, or taxonomy, or categorization, 54
code of ethical conduct, 136
code of ethics, 145
code of responsible business conduct, 152
codes, 102
codes of ethics, 107

commitment, 69
committing acts of personal decadence, 98
common sense, 20, 35
communicate, 161
communication from top to bottom, 5
community, 130, 132
company
    ethics statements or codes, 153
    standards, 2
company's vision/mission statement, 136
compliance, 127, 159
    programs, 127
components of integrity, 127
compromises, 86
compulsion, 66
compulsive quality, 66
conceptions, 52, 53
concepts, 52
conceptual clarity, 25
concerns, 53
condoning unethical actions, 100
conflicting interests, 145
conforming, 14
Confucianism, 125
Confucius, 91
consequentialism, 112
constitutional principles, 146
content, 60
context, 60
convivial institutions, 41

Index

core moral values, 138
core values, 104, 117, 127, 137
corporate
    citizen, 142
    culture, 118
    cultures, 119
    ethics, 150
        codes, 134
        practices, 153
    governance, 119
    mission, 125
    safeguards, 120
corrupt practices, 157
cost-benefit analysis, 112
critical
    ethical factors, 159
    ethical inadequacy, 158
    thinking, 12
    virtues, 159
criticism, 54
cultural
    diversity, 121
    heritage, 124
    identity, 121
    minorities, 120
culture, 118, 119, 139
    of peace, 122
cultures, 124, 125
customer relations, 6
Customer relationship management (CRM), 5

D

Daigneault, Michael, 127, 134
Dalla Costa, 134, 143, 158
decision makers, 44
decision-making, 108
delegation, 34
democracy, 14, 38
    or participation, 11
democratic consultation, 34
deontological, 113
Deontologists, 64
depth, 66
desired ethical action, 107
desires, 64, 70
Deuteronomic demand, 130
dictatorship, 38
dignity, 139, 140, 141, 143
dilemma, 137, 138
dilemmas, 137
direct reports, 1, 2
discipline, 16, 25
    and authority, 23, 31
discipline of reason, 60
distancing, 32
diversity, 124, 126, 142
divisive or elitist, 11
divulging proprietary information, 98

E

economic and social
    development, 155
    impact of business, 155
economic health, 155
educating, 39
    for passion, 72

INDEX

education, 11, 14, 41, 155, 161
   indoctrination, and training;, 43
educational
   system, 124
   theory, 30, 41
educationalists, 28
educator, 51
effective ethics programs, 154
efficiency, 51
egalitarianism, 13
emotional reactions, 58
empathetic, 149
empirical fact, 26
employee
   morale, 127
   opinion surveys, 153
   relations, 6
   safety, 132
   turnover, 6
employer/employee dichotomy, 3
encoding new learning, 160
ends-based thinking, 111
enforcement, 26
Enron, 143
entitlement, 36
envy, 16
eros, 70
ethic, 135
ethical, 144, 160
ethical analysis, 145
ethical and moral education, 132, 133
ethical behavior, 85, 153
   for employees, 159

ethical
   breakdowns, 160
   company, 162
   culture, 119
   decision, 145
   decision-making, 148
   deliberation and decisions, 160
   demands, 129
   dilemma, 95, 145, 146
   dilemmas, 138, 145, 147
   expectations, 158
   implications, 159
   interaction, 159
   issues, 135, 145, 153
   manager, 133
   maturity, 161
   obligations, 129
   organizations, 143, 144
   orientation, 143, 158, 159, 160, 161
   orientation model, 159
   performance, 158
   principles, 127
   problems, 138
   questions, 2
   relativism, 33
   responsibilities, 119
   style, 149
   thing, 157
   thinking in business, 150
   understanding, 160
   violation, 97
   virtue, 158

Index

ethical/moral leadership and management, 89
ethics, 45, 85, 126, 127, 134, 136, 144, 150, 153
    committee, 151
    hot line, 153
    in the workplace, 145, 147
    issues, 136
    offices, 136
    program, 144, 149, 151
    questions, 153
executives, 43
expectations, 6
experience, 69
experts, 3
extremism, 20
extremist phenomena, 33
extremists, 20

F

facilitator, 1
fail, 15
fair economic competition, 142
fair profit, 132, 146
fairness, 121, 122, 134, 135, 141, 155
    and integrity in all dealings, 143
falsely assigning blame, 96
fanaticism, 20
Fascism, 4
fears, 103
feelings, 59

Feuerstein, Aaron, 93
formal instructor, 51
foundational principles, 126
framework, 54
free expression, 72
freedom, 14
    of association, 120
    of information, 120
fundamental guiding principles of the company, 154

G

GATT/World Trade Organization, 156
general principles for business, 154
giving or allowing false impressions, 97
global
    commerce, 156
    corporate citizens, 142
    ethic, 117, 159
    ethics, 123, 124, 125, 126
    issues, 139
globalization, 120
goals, 144
Golden Rule, 56, 125, 157
good faith, 132
good intentions aside, 134
Greenspan, Alan, 128
guilt, 17

H

hard line, 38

INDEX

"Heightened Interest in Ethics Education Reflects Employer, Employee Concerns,", 152
heroes, 92
heuristics, 54
hiding or divulging information, 98
hierarchies, 5
hierarchy, 34
high quality products and services, 143
Hinduism, 125
honesty, 55, 130, 133, 134, 155
    in communications, 143
honesty, morality and conscience, 130
honor obligations, 155
How Good People Make Tough Choices: Resolving the Dilemmas of Ethical Living, 137
HR Magazine, 136
human
    dignity, 126, 139
    rights, 121, 142, 155

I

ideals, 56
identification, 10
    with authority, 10, 12
    with the child, 16
ideology, 12
Immanuel Kant's categorical imperative, 109
immoral, 50
impersonal authority, 14
Implementation Plan for an Ethical Organization, 158
inclusion, 161
individual versus community, 137
industrial espionage, 142
Industrial Revolution, 3
inherent dignity, 126
inspection, 54
integration, 11, 13
integrity, 91, 106, 123, 127, 128, 130, 134, 135, 136, 139, 142, 148, 152
interconnectedness, 126
intrinsic motivation, 41
intuitive, 149
Islamic
    business ethics, 132
    businessperson, 132
It's Good Business: Ethics and Free Enterprise for the New Millennium, 150

J

Jainism, 125
Jewish
    business ethics, 128
    business person, 130
Johnson & Johnson, 88
Judaism, 125
just wage, 132
justice, 55, 121
justice versus mercy, 137

Index

K

Kidder, Rushworth, 137

L

lead by example, 161
leader, 3, 119
leaders, 43
leadership, 161
leading by example, 3
letter of the law, 129
liberation or autonomy, 13
listening to constituencies, 143
local cultures, 142
loss of credibility, 143
Loyalist, 149
loyalty, 143

M

Machiavelli, 91
management, 3, 7, 44, 75, 119, 120, 121, 141, 148, 158
manager, 1, 120
managerial ethics, 136
managers, 2, 43, 157
managing with passion, 73
Marxism, 4
meaning, 66
mental equipment, 46
Merck & Co., 94
method, 54
minorities, 121
misperceptions, 31

models, 137
moderation, 20
modern pressures, 6
Mohammadism, 125
moral, 47
   and ethical nature, 151
   and ethical values in the work place, 151
   beliefs, 59
   character, 101
   content, 11, 46, 59, 60
   corporation, 120
   decision-making model, 145, 147
   education, 9, 11, 43, 119, 127, 130, 131
   education standard, 117
   educator, 118
   integrity, 121
   issues, 46, 48
   management, 7
   manager, 1, 2, 7, 119, 125, 162
   model, 119
   principle, 122
   principles, 56, 146
   quagmire, 3
   qualities, 78
   reasoning, 60, 61
   rules, 150
   values, 119, 146
   virtues, 75
moral/ethical education, 128
morality, 45, 50, 59, 82, 129

Index

morally
    appropriate corporation, 127
    educated, 133
        individual, 127
        manager, 123
motivator, 119
multilateral trade, 156
mutual reflection, 60

N

Nash, Laura, 134
NavPress, 130
New Age ethics, 125
non-rational authority, 37
norm, 102, 119
norms, 120
not-for-profit, 75

O

obedience, 14, 25
objects of passion, 69
obligation
    to the community, 146
    to the stockholders, 106
ombudsmen, 136
ombudsperson, 151
openness in sharing information, 143
orders, 1
organizational systems and decision processes, 161
overriding desires, 70

P

paradigms, 137, 138
Parents, 28
participation, 14, 34, 38
pass, 15
passion, 7, 63
patterns, 137
    of consumption, 124
penalties/consequences and rewards, 161
performance
    appraisals, 158
    evaluations, 153
permitting organizational abuse, 99
perpetrating interpersonal abuse, 99
person's behavior, 56
personal accountability and responsibility, 131
philosophical, 53
philosophy, 40, 53
    of education, 40
    of management or moral theory, 54
    of moral education, 9
Platinum Rule, 157
pluralistic attitude, 122
political correctness, 76
pragmatism, 135
prefects, 27
preferences, 64, 70
pressures, 6

Index

principle of universalisability, 56
principled business leadership, 139
principled/ethical organization, 139
principles, 56, 75, 120, 121, 122, 124, 125, 146, 147, 149
  of morality, 71
privacy, 132, 133
problems, 6
professional, 149
  ethics, 43, 50, 51, 76
profit motive, 75
profit-making organization, 75
profitability, 143
public image, 144
pupils, 28
Puritanism, 17

Q

qualities, 48
  of moral management, 43
quality, 47

R

racism, 58
Rae and Wong, 145
rational authority, 36, 37
rational
  discipline, 36
  stance, 11
rationalizations, 96
reason, 58, 59
reasonable profitability, 131

reasoning, 58, 59
rejection, 10
  of authority, 10
relativism, 12, 13
relevant feelings, 67
reliability, 135
religious
  approach, 131
  tradition, 129, 131
  traditions, 128
resentment, 16
respect, 36, 126, 139, 141, 142, 143, 150
  for rules, 156
  for the environment, 156
respondents, 25
responsibilities of business, 154
responsibility, 134, 158
return
  on investment, 132
  on our owners' investment, 141
reversibility, 113, 126
"right answers", 11, 12
right behavior, 101
"right" value, 103
right versus right, 137, 138, 162
right versus wrong, 137, 138
ritual, 129
  demands, 129
role, 45
rule-based thinking, 112
Rule-Bound, 149

INDEX

S

sanctions, 26
saying things you know are not true, 96
self-discipline, 39
senior management, 158
sense of community, 91
separation or isolation, 34
service, 131, 132
services, 132, 139, 142
shared
    ethical values, 122
        and principles, 125
    values, 154
shareholder, 90
short-term versus long-term, 137
simplistic approaches, 105
slaves, 3
social, 48
    priorities, 124
Socialism, 4
Solomon, Robert C., 149, 150
solutions, 6
spiritual education, 64
stakeholder principles, 154
standards
    of decency, 134
    of professional conduct, 102
Strat-Ethic Plan, 159
subordinate, 3
subordinates, 4
suggestions for improvement, 26
support for multilateral trade, 156
survival, 155

T

taking
    orders, 14
    property, 96
    things that don't belong to you, 96
    unfair advantage, 98
talk the talk, 148
taxonomy, 54
teacher, 51
    education, 39
teachers, 28, 38, 39
teaching, 39
teleological, 112
teleologists, 64
The Conference Board, 153
the environment, 47
the future manager, 82
the language of ethical lapses, 96
the meanings of words, 40
the transmission of values, 43
theory, 54
tolerance of separation, 34
toleration of being separate, 31
Torah, 129, 130
totalitarianism and anarchy, 20
trade secrets, 156
traditions, 133
train, 145, 161
trained, 147
training, 6, 157
    on ethical standards, 136
    workshops, 153
traits, 138

Index

trust, 128, 134, 143, 148, 151
trusted company, 143, 144
trusting
    company, 144
    environment, 144
    work environment, 144
trustworthiness, 123
trustworthy, 144
truth versus loyalty, 137
truthfulness, 141
turnover, 157
12 Building Blocks of Trust, 148
Tylenol product tampering, 88

U

understanding
    and acceptance, 35
     of discipline and authority, 35
unethical
    behavior, 50
    conduct, 107
universal
    concerns and behaviors, 133
    ethic, 117, 121
    global ethics, 127
    intimacy, 84
    moral education, 121, 123
    reasons, 57
universalizability, 126
universalize, 64
unlearning, 158
usury, 48
utilitarian, 149
utilitarian basis, 55
utilitarianism, 111, 112
utilitarians, 64

V

value, 25, 138, 154, 155
values, 119, 120, 121, 124, 125, 136, 144, 154, 159
    education, 43
viability, 155
violating rules, 99
virtue, 69, 91
    ethics, 102
virtues, 50, 56
virtuous, 149
vitalization, 155

W

walk the talk, 148
walk the walk, 148
wants, 64
welfare, 155
Wells, Susan J., 136
White, Jerry, 130
workers, 4
workers and management, 4
world community, 155
world standard, 154
written policy, 145
written standards or codes of ethical business conduct, 136

Z

Zoroasterism, 125

About the Authors

Samuel M. Natale is Professor of Strategic Management, School of Business of Adelphi University, and, concurrently, Senior Research Associate, Department of Educational Studies, at the University of Oxford. Natale is also editor in chief of three international journals which include *International Journal of Value-Based Management; Cross-Cultural Management;* and co-editor of the *International Journal of Effective Board Performance.* His current research focuses on institutional board performance and strategic models for universities and colleges. He received his B.A. degree from LaSalle University, M.A. from the University of Maryland, and D.Phil. from the University of Oxford.

John B. Wilson is an international authority on Moral Education and his philosophical research has spanned decades and is foundational in any discussion of moral education. He is now retired as a Lecturer in Educational Studies at Oxford University as well as from being Fellow of Mansfield College, Oxford. Mr. Wilson has been President of the Philosophical Society of England and has published extensively in the field of religious and moral education.

Linda S. Perry is a business executive with more than 20 years in the field of human resources. She is currently principal and owner of L. Perry Associates, a consulting firm providing solutions for organizations in international human resources management and an adjunct faculty member at C.W. Post/Long Island University, where she teaches a number of business courses. Previously, Ms. Perry was Sr. Vice President of Human Resources for General Semiconductor, Inc., a global semiconductor manufacturing firm. She has developed and implemented a multitude of domestic and international human resources programs and has facilitated training programs in eight countries.

She holds a bachelor of science degree in human development from the State University of New York and a M.B.A. from Dowling College. She is currently pursuing a Ph.D. in Business Administration from Kennedy-Western University.

A paper she researched and co-authored entitled, *The Literacy Journey...It Continues*, was presented at Oxford University's Centre for the Study of Values in Education and Business and published by the University Press of America, Inc. An article she co-authored, *Empowered Learners: The New Paradigm for 2000 and Beyond*, will be published by the International Journal of Value-Based Management in January, 2002.

Ms. Perry has recently been selected to appear in the International Biographical Centre's publication, *2000 Outstanding Intellectuals of the 21st Century* and the American Biographical Institute's 10th Commemorative Edition of *2,000 Notable American Women*, in recognition of past achievements and outstanding service to community, state, and nation.

Ms. Perry currently resides in New York with her husband, Robert M. Ruggiano.